W9-CFJ-396

At Issue

| Do Students Have Too
| Much Homework?

Other Books in the At Issue Series:

At Issue

Do Students Have Too Much Homework?

Judeen Bartos, Book Editor

GREENHAVEN PRESS
A part of Gale, Cengage Learning

Detroit • New York • San Francisco • New Haven, Conn • Waterville, Maine • London

Elizabeth Des Chenes, *Managing Editor*

© 2012 Greenhaven Press, a part of Gale, Cengage Learning

Gale and Greenhaven Press are registered trademarks used herein under license.

For more information, contact:
Greenhaven Press
27500 Drake Rd.
Farmington Hills, MI 48331-3535
Or you can visit our Internet site at gale.cengage.com

For product information and technology assistance, contact us at

Gale Customer Support, 1-800-877-4253
For permission to use material from this text or product, submit all requests online at www.cengage.com/permissions

Further permissions questions can be emailed to permissionrequest@cengage.com

Articles in Greenhaven Press anthologies are often edited for length to meet page requirements. In addition, original titles of these works are changed to clearly present the main thesis and to explicitly indicate the author's opinion. Every effort is made to ensure that Greenhaven Press accurately reflects the original intent of the authors. Every effort has been made to trace the owners of copyrighted material.

Cover image copyright © Todd Davidson/Illustration works/Corbis.

LIBRARY OF CONGRESS CATALOGING-IN-PUBLICATION DATA

Do students have too much homework? / Judeen Bartos, book editor.
  p. cm. -- (At issue)
Includes bibliographical references and index.
  ISBN 978-0-7377-5892-4 (hardcover) -- ISBN 978-0-7377-5893-1 (pbk.)
  1. Homework. 2. Homework--Cross-cultural studies. I. Bartos, Judeen.
  LB1048.D6 2012
  371.3028'1--dc23

                                                                    2011038304

Printed in the United States of America
2 3 4 5 6 7 16 15 14 13 12

Contents

Introduction

Students, parents, teachers, administrators, and other interested parties all seem to have strong feelings on the subject of homework. Students complain they get too much work to complete outside of the hours they already attend classes. Parents worry their children may not get accepted into college without a rigorous amount of schoolwork. Teachers and administrators feel the pressure from all sides to make sure every child succeeds, and realize they too are being graded accordingly. Perhaps a more important issue is what society expects students will gain from homework and school in general, and not what the recommended workload is that will potentially guarantee achievement.

Within the past two decades, but especially since the passage of the No Child Left Behind Act in 2001, the academic achievement level of American students has been under increased scrutiny. The demand to demonstrate achievement through standardized testing has resulted in pressure on schools, teachers, and students to master more academic content in shorter time periods. Test results often are used as the sole means of judging success, and test performance is being used to allocate funds to schools, review individual teacher performance, and determine college acceptance.

Homework is viewed by many educators as an accepted method to increase student achievement. The "more is better" theory is unquestioned by a majority of school districts. But evidence does not support this philosophy as student test scores remain stagnant. Results from the National Assessment of Educational Progress (NAEP) reveal that in state after state test results have shown little change in the past decade. Moreover, an analysis conducted by David Conley for the Bill and Melinda Gates Foundation in 2007 estimated that up to 40 percent of new college students need at least one remedial course upon entering college. Clearly increasing the amount of homework students are given is not having the desired effect.

A growing chorus of critics is questioning not only standard homework practice, but the real purpose of America's educational system as well. Education expert Tony Wagner offers his analysis of the situation in his book, *The Global Achievement Gap: Why Even Our Best Schools Don't Teach the New Survival Skills Our Children Need—And What We Can Do About It.* Wagner contends that American schools are not teaching the types of skills students will need to succeed not only in college but also in life. An emphasis on memorizing facts and focusing on test preparation is doing students a great disservice, Wagner believes, essentially leaving them unprepared for life after school when critical-thinking and problem-solving skills will be in great demand among potential employers.

And it is not only in the workplace that students will suffer. Wagner asks, "What does it mean in today's world to be an active and informed citizen and how does a democratic society best educate its citizenship?" Students unprepared to analyze problems and reach thoughtful, educated conclusions are not equipped to participate in a democracy, thus weakening the foundation of American society.

It could be that the amount of homework students receive matters less than what may be missing from it—lessons that require students to develop research and analytical skills and the ability to effectively communicate their results. "The rigor that matters most for the twenty-first century is demonstrated mastery of the core competencies for work, citizenship, and life-long learning. Studying academic content is the means of developing competencies, instead of being the goal, as it has been traditionally. In today's world, it's no longer how much you know that matters; it's what you can do with what you know," according to Wagner.

Wagner is not alone in his insight into what it will take for students to succeed in the future. Daniel H. Pink, the author of several bestselling books, including *A Whole New Mind: Why Right-Brainers Will Rule the Future* and *Drive: The Surprising Truth About What Motivates Us*, provides a thought-provoking analysis of what type of learning will be essential to success. Pink believes that "knowledge" workers—computer programmers, engineers and accountants among others—that have dominated our recent history, will shrink in importance. Technology and overseas competition will lessen their value as the future will belong to a different kind of mind—a mind based more on creativity, inventiveness, and big-picture capabilities.

Pink believes that a large part of what humans can accomplish is based on motivation, and that motivation comes more from intrinsic satisfaction than external rewards. Schools that heavily rely on rote memorization and feedback based on test results may be de-motivating students and leading them to dislike school and the learning process. Pink writes in *Drive*, "In our offices and our classrooms we have way too much compliance and way too little engagement." He believes we need to help kids both at home and school "move toward autonomy, mastery and purpose."

Homework assignments, according to Pink, should engage students and offer them some control over how they will master a skill. He writes, "Does the homework bulging from kids' backpacks truly help them learn? Or does it simply steal their free time in the service of a false sense of rigor?" In a future where technological advances are eliminating many of the tasks that used to be done by people, it is imperative that students are taught a new set of skills based on flexibility and creativity, using curiosity and initiative to confront whatever they may encounter. As Pink suggests "With a little thought and effort, we can turn home*work* into home*learning*." The viewpoints in *At Issue: Do Students Have Too Much Homework?* reflect this and other perspectives on this passionately debated topic.

1

Excessive Homework Strains Family Life

Wendy J. Ponte

Wendy J. Ponte is a writer and contributing editor at Mothering *magazine.*

Attitudes in the United States have fluctuated in recent decades about the value of homework. The level of work outside the classroom has seen a decided increase but the negative effects of this rise may outweigh any benefits. Family life is impacted when students receive large amounts of homework to complete each night. Little time is left for family activities and parents feel the stress of either helping children complete the work or policing them to make sure they do it on their own. Chores, exercise, sleep, and just time to play all take a backseat as academic performance becomes the only priority. Parents worry about confronting teachers and schools but when homework policies and practices are adjusted, the results can be positive as children tend to enjoy school more while also demonstrating higher achievement levels. Less is more when it comes to homework.

"Anna woke up this morning so happy because this is a rare weekend where she has very little homework," says her mother, Isabel Hill, of Brooklyn, New York. "Usually, the weekends just go by in a blur of homework. The last two, we've been working from dawn until dusk." School nights are worse. "Anna takes a 30-minute break when she gets home, then she starts her homework and doesn't finish until 10 or 10:30." Anna is in the sixth grade and, according to her mother, she has never *not* had homework—even in kindergarten.

Elizabeth Jones's 17-year-old daughter, Julia, is, as she says, "a very together kid," one of those children who has always gotten straight A's and completed her assignments without a fuss. But this year, in 11th grade, Julia is frequently up until 1 a.m. "It has been an unhappy year because she doesn't have a moment to breathe," says her mother.

A 2002 survey reported that 64 percent of children between the ages of six and eight have homework on any given day—twice what the workload was in 1981. In 2008, even preschoolers are bringing schoolwork home.

Anna's mother feels that homework has reduced her child's desire to learn. Ella's mother reports that her daughter "hopes she can get into a college where learning is fun again."

When is there time to hang out with friends, play a spontaneous game of soccer, write in a diary?

Many parents wonder—how do we reconcile the messages we receive from politicians about the importance of family togetherness with mandates for more and more homework?

When Isabel Hill speaks of her daughter's struggles with homework, it is notable that she often speaks about the work as if it is her own: "the last two [weekends], we've been working from dawn until dusk." Homework impacts everyone in the family, and few elementary and middle-school children are able to manage the planning required to complete the work without considerable help from a parent. Worse, many experts wonder if kids are missing out on a real childhood. When is there time to hang out with friends, play a spontaneous game of soccer, write in a diary?

Common Misperceptions

Proponents of homework list compelling-sounding reasons for its importance—and some can tell you why they think there should be even more of it. Here are some of them:

Homework improves academic ability. Doing more work will make children learn more than they could within school hours.

This is refuted by two recent books: *The Case Against Homework: How Homework Is Hurting Children and What Parents Can Do About It,* by Sara Bennett and Nancy Kalish; and *The Homework Myth: Why Our Kids Get Too Much of a Bad Thing,* by Alfie Kohn. The authors state that, to date, no research has supported a correlation between amounts of homework and increased achievement in elementary school. This was also largely true of middle school. Even in high school, where some benefits were evident, these disappeared when too much work was assigned. In fact, too much homework in high school can actually *reduce* academic achievement.

Repetition creates strength. Performing a skill over and over again causes the learning to stick like glue in the child's brain.

This type of homework is often seen in the math worksheets that children bring home: two pages of division problems to solve. For spelling, a child may be asked to write vocabulary words over ten times each.

But, again, no studies back up the claim. There is some indication that repetition can help a child to master skills if the concept behind the skill is already clearly in place, particularly in math. But according to the US Department of Education (DOE), five algebraic problems are all it takes to demonstrate whether or not a child understands a particular mathematical function. When kids come home with 100 multiplication problems to solve, it becomes simple drudgery. As Bennett and Kalish say in their book, the children who already know how to solve the math problem don't need that much practice, and those who don't won't know how to solve it anyway—so why try 100 times?

In fact, the greatest arguments against repetitive homework, and homework that requires mere rote memorization, are that it does not require children to think creatively, does not instill a love of learning, and strongly contributes to their disliking school altogether.

Homework teaches kids responsibility and improves organizational skills. If given plenty of work to do at home, children will need to budget their time in order to complete it. They will also get used to the idea of sitting down and just getting things done—a valuable tool for future success.

"Such a claim might be plausible," says Alfie Kohn in *The Homework Myth*, "until we stop to ask what it is, exactly, for which students are actually responsible. Almost never are they permitted to decide whether to have homework, or how much, or what kind. Instead, their choices are limited to such peripheral questions as when to do what they've been required to do." One mother Kohn interviewed said that what homework assignments really test is *her* proficiency at budgeting time.

Nor do many schools spend any significant classroom time teaching kids how to organize work and manage their time—training that could also prepare children for the greater homework loads in higher grades.

Homework is a great way for parents to see what their kids are doing in school. Furthermore, homework can promote greater closeness between parent and child.

Tensions over homework, however, are the evening scenario in all too many homes. After a long day at work, many parents understandably resent having to play Homework Cop, nor do they need any more issues over which to butt heads with their kids. Can parents just as easily find out what their children are doing by talking with their kids about school and by looking at some of their work?

As well, assigning a lot of homework may not be equitable. Not all parents are able to provide enough time and attention to help their children with homework, and/or an environment conducive to completing it. Less wealthy parents may work more than one job. Single mothers may have divided attentions. And some parents may not even speak English.

"I don't think it is fair to assess homework when I can't be sure that the child's home environment is supportive," says fourth-grade teacher Allegra Love, who works in a bilingual school in Santa Fe, New Mexico. Love gives her kids a nightly journal prompt that takes about 20 minutes to complete. Many of the other fourth-grade teachers in her school give several hours of homework.

Free time is just as likely to create opportunities for unexpected learning.

Homework keeps kids out of trouble. If children are left with too much time on their hands, they won't spend it wisely, and are certain to waste it on video games and television—or worse.

Alfie Kohn thinks that much of modern-day education is infused with this mindset, which, he writes, reveals a deep societal distrust of children, particularly teenagers. Traditional classroom education seeks to control how children behave, what they think, and exactly what they learn. In fact, Kohn says, there is an almost puritanical belief that because kids don't like doing homework, it *must* be good for them. But, as Kohn also points out, "[I]f we don't trust our children to stay out of trouble, then trying to keep them busy is unlikely to accomplish this goal. Whatever our kids are doing says more about our relationship with them than it does about how much free time they have." Free time is just as likely to create opportunities for unexpected learning, Kohn thinks, and is also the best way to spark new ideas.

"I Don't Remember Having Any Homework at All!"

I've heard this from most parents I've spoken to about homework. What has changed? Why is so much more homework now given at such early ages?

The belief in homework's benefits has ebbed and flowed over the years. Most experts agree that the launch of the Soviet [Union (USSR)] satellite Sputnik in 1957 caused changes in education that still reverberate today. Shocked and dismayed by the USSR's ability to produce scientists who could design and launch a satellite before the US could, experts called for more rigorous educational practices and, especially, more homework. In 1983, *A Nation at Risk* [by the National Commission on Excellence in Education] cried out against mediocrity in American education. The DOE responded by stating that homework is an essential part of a good education.

Alfie Kohn thinks there is even more to it than that. "Homework, I'll argue, is a field on which much larger disputes are played out, including those involving standardized testing, the characteristics of good pedagogy, the nature and purposes of education, our attitudes toward research, and the ways we raise and regard children."

Some other factors include:

College Expectations. The main reason for the intense pressure exerted on children in most high schools is the looming presence of college. Getting into a good college—we aren't even talking the Ivy League here—is *very* competitive. To be accepted into one of the better schools, kids are expected to not only have straight A's, but also to do volunteer work, play sports, travel, write at a college level, participate in school politics, and more.

While good "family values" is one of the qualities that can help a student get into college, few ambitious teenagers these days can spend significant amounts of quality time with their families—because of how much homework they must complete.

The main reason for the intense pressure exerted on children in most high schools is the looming presence of college.

Grade Inflation. The pressure to please college admissions boards and score well on standardized tests has changed the meanings of high-school letter grades. In his article "Whatever Happened to the *Average* Student?," education speaker Tom Krause says that "When I was in school a 'C' grade meant normal.[...] Just like the disappearing middle class, the place for the average student seems to be fading away in today's educational setting."

"It's not just about learning anymore—it's about *doing well*," says mother Elizabeth Jones. "Kids are stuck in this race. Teachers give them grief for grade grubbing and lobbying—but without the grade, they can't get into a good school."

State Testing and Funding. The Organization for Economic Co-operation and Development's Programme for International Student Assessment is a triennial survey that measures reading, mathematical, and scientific literacy of the world's teenagers. Of 15-year-old students tested in 57 countries, those in Finland earned the highest science scores. But according to a recent article in the *Wall Street Journal*, Finnish students rarely have more than a half hour of homework, there are no honor societies, no stress over college entrance (in Finland, college is free), and no "gifted" classes—and, needless to say, kindergartners never get homework. In fact, Finnish children don't start school until age seven. What's different there?

"What they find is simple but not easy: well-trained teachers and responsible children. Early on, kids do a lot without adults hovering. And teachers create lessons to fit their students," reports the *Wall Street Journal*. Rather than pushing gifted students ahead, the focus is placed on teaching weaker students.

In the US, the No Child Left Behind (NCLB) Act of 2001 has helped create a very different approach. In this controversial program, designed to provide incentives for improving education, each state is mandated to prove that children are achieving academically before it can receive federal funding for schools. The atmosphere created by this need to prove academic accomplishment, usually via standardized tests, is fraught. Critics of NCLB say that it has contributed to "teaching to the test" rather than focusing on truly valuable learning tools.

Some experts think that the homework problem is deeply woven into the very fabric of our system of educating children.

The Belief That More Is Better. In the Joneses' children's advanced-placement (AP) classes, reports their mother, there is an almost "macho" sense that, when it comes to the homework load, more is better. The "more" tends to be a greater volume of work rather than more challenging work. "On Tuesday, [Julia] was assigned [to read] two essays by [Ralph] Ellison, each around 20 pages long. She was then told to write two three-page papers on these essays—due Thursday." And this is just the homework for one class.

Alfie Kohn has studied the ways in which competition affects learning. "Study after study has found that when we're involved in some sort of contest we end up not doing as well on most tasks as we would in the absence of competition," he says. In an attempt to create more learning by spending more time doing homework, students may actually be learning *less* than they are capable of.

Sexism Against Boys? Caroline Thaler is a mother and educator who was a teacher and an assistant principal in the New York City Public School System. She now works for Australian and United States Services In Education (AUSSIE), a company dedicated to creating better school curricula. Thaler thinks that gender is a big factor in how well today's kids do in school. Many boys succeed academically, but she feels that, in general, girls are stronger in some skills that make it easier to be a "good" student, such as paying attention to details, sitting still, or homing in on what the teacher is looking for.

Curricula. Some experts think that the homework problem is deeply woven into the very fabric of our system of educating children. Are the curricula that most schools use fostering learning or "behaviors"?

"What happens in most middle and high schools is that homework is the overflow," says Thaler. "There is no way that teachers can begin to get enough real work done in a 45-minute class." Deduct the time it takes kids to sit down, get organized, and then pack up again at the end, and that leaves only about 35 minutes of actual teaching time. What can't get done in that time is sent home.

Thaler believes in the workshop model. "You can't learn by just being *told* something and then going off and doing it," she says. "You learn by repeated modeling and guided support." Longer class times can facilitate this type of learning.

Because of Homework, What Is *Not* Getting Done?

Many parents are equally upset by the experiences their children are *not* getting because of mounting pressure to perform in school:

Chores. Many proponents of homework suggest that doing schoolwork at home teaches kids a sense of responsibility. "I'd rather have them learning responsibility from chores," counters Thaler. But if her children are already staying up late doing

19

homework, how can she then ask them to stay up even later to wash the dishes? Some parents have the sense that they are servants or valets to their children, who should be learning to do their own laundry but don't have time to fit it in.

Sleep. According to the National Sleep Foundation, children from 5 to 12 years old need between 10 and 11 hours of sleep each night. Teenagers need from 8.5 to 9.25 hours. But when teens get overwhelmed with schoolwork, sleep is one of the first things to go. Studies show that only 20 percent of adolescents between the ages of 11 and 17 get the recommended amount of sleep. On school nights, nearly half of them sleep fewer than eight hours.

Research shows that sleep deprivation affects a whole range of mental activities, including the ability to pay attention, verbal creativity, abstract thinking, decision making, retrieval of long-term memories, and overall mood and motivation. Researchers have also found that when a person learns something new, there is activity during sleep in the same area of the brain where that learning occurred, and improvement in memory performance when the person is tested the next day. Sufficient sleep, it turns out, is crucial to assimilating new information.

Downtime and Play. Recently, there has been increasing interest in studying the purpose of play. Some studies on rats reveal that major surges in cerebellum growth correspond with peak levels of playtime. Researchers are wondering if this correlates with how children's brains respond to play.

One thing is for sure—overworked kids don't get to play much. Whereas teenagers tend to sacrifice sleep when they have a lot of homework, for younger school-age children, it is fun time and social activities that end up being sacrificed. The long-term effects of lack of play are as yet unknown.

Exercise. Play also means movement. Kids who don't have time for play and recreational activities, such as softball teams or dance, just don't get to move around a lot—and there is evidence that exercise actually helps with academics. "While study after study shows that homework has no or little effect on kids' overall achievement until high school, a review of 850 studies by the [Centers for Disease Control and Prevention] showed that physical activity has a positive impact on everything from grade point average, scores on standardized tests, and grades in specific courses to concentration, memory, and classroom behavior," write Bennett and Kalish.

Socializing. Time to socialize is something Isabel Hill wants badly for her daughter, Anna. During my interview with her, when I mentioned that my own daughter was going to the corner to have pizza with a friend, she said, wistfully, "My God, wouldn't it be nice if Anna could go out for pizza with a friend on a weekday."

For children, socializing with their peers is truly a laboratory for learning. It is in these situations, unsupervised by adults and not organized by teachers or coaches, where they learn what works and does not work in human relations.

Extracurricular Activities. "Anna has always loved music," says Hill. "We've had to really compromise with that because she just doesn't have the time. It's a travesty, because music is a lifelong pleasure."

It is said that when Thomas Jefferson had writer's block, he would stop and, to revitalize his creativity, play his violin. This is just one example of how a broad range of activities and interests can improve a student's performance in school.

Family Time and Privacy. Imagine taking a job where you are told: "Work is over at 6:00 p.m. However, we also supervise your time at home and on vacations. We will make sure that you leave the office every night with a minimum of three hours of paperwork to do, and if we can't find something that really needs to get done, we'll make something up. And, sure, you can go on vacation if you like. We'll even cut back on the busywork—a bit. And, by the way, you will be paid nothing for this, and you can't quit this job."

It sounds ridiculous, but it is real life for many children. "Over Christmas, there was a project and a paper due at the end of the break," reports Elizabeth Jones. "This had to be done with two class partners. Two of Julia's partners had gone away—one of them to Mexico—so there was a huge scramble to do this over the phone long-distance, and then finish it up the last day before school started up."

But do schools have the right to dictate what our children can and cannot do once they've left school? Do they have the right to decide how much time we will spend with our children on evenings and weekends—even on vacation?

Here in the US, we get a lot of mixed messages about family life. We are encouraged by politicians to get back to basics and make sure to have more family meals. Jones and her husband have worked hard to keep this up in their family. But the moment dinner is over, her kids jump up to get back to their homework. "That 20-minute meal is all we get with them," she says. "It's very sad."

A New Approach Is Needed

"Questioning the amount of homework should just be the beginning," Alfie Kohn told me. "But much of it isn't worth two minutes of time, never mind an hour."

Mandating "no homework" days or weekends, or setting guidelines for how much time children should spend on homework according to their ages, may seem a good beginning, but such policies are too easy to bypass. At the Jones kids' high school, the AP teachers simply ignore "no homework" nights. After all, if you're in an AP class, then you're expected to behave like a college student and tough it out.

In his book, Kohn questions the current position of homework as the "default." Why, he wonders, are we in the position of having to prove that all this homework is not beneficial? Why aren't teachers and school administrators expected to prove that it *is*? Couldn't teachers assign homework only on those rare occasions when the work really can't be accomplished at school—as in, say, a project for which a child is interviewing various people on a certain topic?

Most homework experts suggest that it is better to approach a school in a group than individually.

It's hard for parents to be voices for change in their children's schools. Many fear that their activism against school practices will negatively affect their children's experience at school. Maybe the teachers will be tougher on their kids—maybe the parents' "tirades" will even affect their kids' grades.

Most homework experts suggest that it is better to approach a school in a group than individually. Caroline Thaler, who has had some success in effecting change at her own children's school, says, "It's easy to swat at one fly, but less easy to remove an entire swarm of them."

In 2005, after a revamping of its curriculum, the Banks County Middle School, in Homer, Georgia, stopped assigning regular homework. It was felt that homework was setting kids up for failure and causing them to feel badly about school. The results have been stunning: Grades are up dramatically, and results on statewide tests are rising rapidly.

The Kino School, in Tucson, Arizona, has a different approach to homework: "We give the students ample time to do their work during the school day," says Mary Jane Cera, the school's director. "Oftentimes children, especially the high schoolers, prefer to socialize during that time and bring work home instead." This, she feels, teaches time management in a much more positive way because it is about choice, and at Kino, choice is a keystone of education. "We've never wavered in our belief about respecting children," declares Cera.

As far as homework is concerned, that might just say it all.

2

College Students Study Less Than in the Past

Keith O'Brien

Keith O'Brien is a former Boston Globe *reporter and winner of the Casey Medal for Meritorious Journalism in 2009. His work has appeared in* Boston Magazine, Runner's World, *and* The Scientist. *He has contributed stories to several National Public Radio shows including* Here and Now, Weekend America, *and* Only a Game.

College students appear to be studying far fewer hours than in the past, according to an analysis of time-use surveys taken since 1961. Two California economics professors conducted the research which shows that this decline can be found at all levels— undergraduate, graduate, and doctoral—and all types and sizes of programs. The researchers and other experts offer several theories for their results but are not able to pinpoint why time spent studying decreased. Technological distractions, more students working while attending college, and a breakdown of the relationship between professor and student are all seen by some to be contributing factors. Although some may question if time spent studying is even as relevant as it was fifty years ago, others wonder if today's students are really receiving the preparation they will need to succeed after graduation.

They come with polished resumes and perfect SAT scores. Their grades are often impeccable. Some elite universities will deny thousands of high school seniors with 4.0 grade point averages in search of an elusive quality that one provost called "intellectual vitality." The perception is that today's over-achieving, college-driven kids have it—whatever it is. They're not just groomed; they're ready. There's just one problem.

Once on campus, the students aren't studying.

It is a fundamental part of college education: the idea that young people don't just learn from lectures, but on their own, holed up in the library with books and, perhaps, a trusty yellow highlighter. But new research, conducted by two California economics professors, shows that over the past five decades, the number of hours that the average college student studies each week has been steadily dropping. According to time-use surveys analyzed by professors Philip Babcock, at the University of California Santa Barbara, and Mindy Marks, at the University of California Riverside, the average student at a four-year college in 1961 studied about 24 hours a week. Today's average student hits the books for just 14 hours.

The decline, Babcock and Marks found, infects students of all demographics. No matter the student's major, gender, or race, no matter the size of the school or the quality of the SAT scores of the people enrolled there, the results are the same: Students of all ability levels are studying less.

In survey after survey since 2000, college and high school students are alarmingly candid that they are simply not studying very much at all.

"It's not just limited to bad schools," Babcock said. "We're seeing it at liberal arts colleges, doctoral research colleges, masters colleges. Every different type, every different size. It's just across the spectrum. It's very robust. This is just a huge change in every category."

The research, accepted to be published in the *Review of Economics and Statistics*, has already sparked discussions in faculty lounges and classrooms across the country. Some question whether college students ever could have studied 24 hours a week—roughly three and a half hours a night. But even if you dispute the historical decline, there is still plenty of reason for concern over the state of 21st-century study practices. In survey after survey since 2000, college and high school students are alarmingly candid that they are simply not studying very much at all. Some longtime professors have noted the trend, which rarely gets mentioned by college admissions officials when prospective students visit campus.

Simple Answers Are Not Apparent

But when it comes to "why," the answers are less clear. The easy culprits—the allure of the Internet (Facebook!), the advent of new technologies (dude, what's a card catalog?), and the changing demographics of college campuses—don't appear to be driving the change, Babcock and Marks found. What might be causing it, they suggest, is the growing power of students and professors' unwillingness to challenge them.

Whatever the reason, one thing is clear: The central bargain of a college education—that students have fairly light classloads because they're independent enough to be learning outside the classroom—can no longer be taken for granted. And some institutions of higher learning have yet to grapple with, or even accept, the possibility that something dramatic has happened.

Studying has long been considered a key part of a college student's growth, both as a means to an end—a deeper understanding of the subject matter—and as a valuable habit in its own right. A person who can self-motivate to learn, academics argue, is not only more likely to be a productive worker, but more fulfilled citizen. As a result, universities for decades have stated—sometimes officially—that for every hour students spend in class each week they are expected to be studying for two hours on their own.

"So if students are taking a full load of 15 credit hours, they should be studying for 30 hours," said Jillian Kinzie, the associate director of the National Survey of Student Engagement, a nonprofit at Indiana University. "Clearly, that's not happening."

One problem is that they're arriving in college with increasingly troubled study habits. According to survey data gathered by the Cooperative Institutional Research Program, or CIRP, the largest and longest-running study of higher education in the United States, incoming college freshmen have reported declining study habits for at least two decades. By 2009, nearly two-thirds of them failed to study even six hours a week while seniors in high school—a figure that has risen steadily since 1987.

Once they get to college, the figure improves, but there are many students today who appear to be doing very little whatsoever. In one CIRP survey subset last year, analyzing predominantly private institutions considered to be mid-level or high-achieving colleges, some 32 percent of college freshmen somehow managed to study less than six hours a week—not even an hour a day. Seniors studied only slightly more, with nearly 28 percent studying less than six hours a week. And other surveys of today's students report similarly alarming results. The National Survey of Student Engagement found in 2009 that 62 percent of college students studied 15 hours a week or less—even as they took home primarily As and Bs on their report cards.

"Are students just that much more efficient that more than 60 percent of students study less than 15 hours a week and still earn As and Bs?" Kinzie asked. "Or are we really preparing students for the world of work if they're able to get by spending that many hours studying and preparing for class?"

More Interests Compete for Students' Time

Critics say it's misleading to measure today's students by the number of hours they spend studying. Students live very different lives than they once did. They are more likely to hold down jobs while attending classes.

John Bravman, vice provost for undergraduate education at Stanford University, said that what he worries about these days is not that students are lazy, but that they are too busy—busier than previous generations of Stanford students.

"Much busier," Bravman said, describing the "on-demand" world that students work in today. "I was a student here from '75 to '79. I was reasonably engaged in things. But I had so much free time compared to students today. They do so many things—it's amazing."

According to the skeptics of the findings, there is one other notable change: Today's students are working with more efficient tools when they do finally sit down to study. They don't have to bang out a term paper on a typewriter; nor do they need to wander the stacks at the library for hours, tracking down some dusty tome.

"A student doesn't need to retype a paper three times before handing it in," said Heather Rowan-Kenyon, an assistant professor of higher education at Boston College. "And a student today can sit on their bed and go to the library, instead of going to the library and going to the card catalog."

That's true, Babcock and Marks agree. But according to their research, the greatest decline in student studying took place before computers swept through colleges: Between 1961 and 1981, study times fell from 24.4 to 16.8 hours per week (and then, ultimately, to 14). Nor do they believe student employment or changing demographics to be the root cause. While they acknowledge that students are working more and campuses attract students who wouldn't have bothered attending college a generation ago, the researchers point out that study times are dropping for everyone regardless of employment or personal characteristics.

"It's pretty shocking," said Marks, who is concerned about the trend.

Hours spent studying is not the end goal of an education, of course, nor the only way to determine if someone is learning or will land a job after college. Marks herself points out that employers don't generally care about the content of job applicants' classes; they're more interested in whether an applicant graduated, was able to meet deadlines, and work within a bureaucracy.

But one sign that studying still has value is that students themselves are concerned about it. In a 2008 survey of more than 160,000 undergraduates enrolled in the University of California system, students were asked to list what interferes most with their academic success. Some blamed family responsibilities, some blamed jobs. The second most common obstacle to success, according to the students, was that they were depressed, stressed, or upset. And then came the number one reason, agreed upon by 33 percent of students, who said they struggled with one particular problem "frequently" or "all the time": They simply did not know how to sit down and study.

One sign that studying still has value is that students themselves are concerned about it.

Changes Drive Down Rigor

So what now? Given Babcock and Marks's findings, what should universities be doing to improve study habits? It's an answer that depends, first, on understanding why students are studying so little these days. And on this point, there is little agreement.

One theory, offered by Babcock and Marks, suggests that the cause, or at least one of them, is a breakdown in the professor-student relationship. Instead of a dynamic where a professor sets standards and students try to meet them, the more common scenario these days, they suggest, is one in which both sides hope to do as little as possible.

"No one really has an incentive to make a demanding class," Marks said. "To make a tough assignment, you have to write it, grade it. Kids come into office hours and want help on it. If you make it too hard, they complain. Other than the sheer love for knowledge and the desire to pass it on to the next generation, there is no incentive in the system to encourage effort."

The problem dates back to the 1960s, said Murray Sperber, a visiting professor in the graduate school of education at the University of California Berkeley. Sperber, at the time, was a graduate student at Berkeley and was part of an upstart movement pushing for students to rate their professors. The idea, Sperber said, was to give students a chance to express their opinions about their classes—a noble thought, but one that has backfired, according to many professors. Course evaluations have created a sort of "nonaggression pact," Sperber said, where professors—especially ones seeking tenure—go easy on the homework and students, in turn, give glowing course evaluations.

No one really has an incentive to make a demanding class.

In response to these concerns over course evaluations—and the state of collegiate studying in general—some universities are making changes. Some administrators in recent years have been putting less weight on course evaluations when making tenure decisions. Professors are being told to give explicit tasks to students. Just telling them to read these days is often considered "too generic, too general of a request," said Kinzie. And many professors today are using Internet-based systems, like Blackboard, where students are required to log on and write about the assigned reading for all of their classmates to see.

Dan Bernstein, director of the Center for Teaching Excellence at Kansas University, said such assignments can help ensure that students are reading and will come prepared for class. But as the Babcock/Marks survey shows, universities aren't coming close to meeting their own expectations for what should be happening on campus. "That," said Bernstein, "is one of our dirty little secrets."

It's possible that college administrators simply don't know what's happening—or rather, not happening—in their dormitories, libraries, and classrooms. The decline in study hours, according to the new research, has happened gradually over decades. Perhaps, some professors argue, colleges simply don't know the extent of the problem—and perhaps a discussion of the new research will lead to positive changes. But there is also a more troubling reason why the study habits of today's students remain a discussion held in private, or not at all.

"If we let it be known that they're not doing their part, that they're not the students of yore, that makes everybody uncomfortable," said Bernstein, a professor of psychology who's been teaching for 35 years. "Our constituents—our stakeholders, as they call them—would be unhappy. They like to prefer that we're doing our jobs well."

3

Schools Need to Reduce Academic Pressure on Students

Jerusha Conner, Denise Pope, and Mollie Galloway

Jerusha Conner is an assistant professor of education at Villanova University in Pennsylvania. Denise Pope is a senior lecturer at the Stanford University School of Education in California. Mollie Galloway is the director of research and assessment at Lewis and Clark Graduate School in Portland, Oregon.

Several recent studies point to an alarming trend of increased stress among students caused by excessive amounts of homework. The health and well-being of children is threatened by the increased pressure to perform academically. Even those students who appear to be thriving—those who possess higher grade point averages and participate in extra-curricular activities—report that school related factors cause the most stress in their lives. Schools need to recognize the distressed state of their students and work to enact policies and strategies to alleviate it. Even small changes can make a big difference. Adjustments such as adding more downtime during the school day, providing additional tutorial assistance, and eliminating some exams in favor of projects can go a long way toward reducing the anxiety in students' academic lives.

Jerusha Conner, Denise Pope, and Mollie Galloway, "Success with Less Stress," *Educational Leadership*, vol. 67, no. 4, December 2009/January 2010, pp. 54–58. Copyright © 2009 by ASCD (Association for Supervision and Curriculum Development). All rights reserved. Reprinted with permission of the publisher. Learn more about ASCD at www.ascd.org.

Students with high grade point averages often carry an unhealthy load of stress. How can schools help?

The headlines are alarming. Many students who feel the pressure to succeed have been cheating, pulling all nighters to study, becoming depressed, and seeking relief in drug use and self-mutilation. Multiple news reports have directed attention to what some are calling an epidemic of student stress in top U.S. schools. These headlines are not just media hype; empirical data corroborate the reports.

Our study explored what students themselves said about the causes of their school-related stress and then looked at ways to reduce it. We hoped to find ways for schools to reverse this trend by developing healthier school environments that promote student engagement and well-being.

Students' responses demonstrated that many feel that school work dominates their day.

From 2006 to 2008, we gathered data from 3,645 students, attending seven high-performing high schools in the California Bay Area. These students appear to be exemplars. The vast majority (85 percent) reported a grade point average of 3.0 or higher, and most (63 percent) reported that they often or always work hard in school. They value achievement and care about learning. In addition, 89 percent participate in an extracurricular activity after school, and most aspire to attend a four-year college. By most indicators, these are the kinds of students we would like our high schools to produce.

A different story emerges, however, from our data. Many students reported feeling stressed out, overworked, and sleep deprived. They spoke of the tolls of stress on their mental and physical well-being and on their ability to learn academic material. Ultimately, their comments raise questions about whether a student's grade point average, frequently used as a marker of student success, is a good indicator of what students are actually learning and accomplishing.

School Worries Are Commonplace Among Students

Science has long recognized that some level of stress can be adaptive and even healthy, however, chronic student stress has been consistently associated with negative outcomes. For the majority of students in this study, academic stress is constant. More than 70 percent of students reported that they often or always feel stressed by their schoolwork, and 56 percent reported often or always worrying about such things as grades, tests, and college acceptance.

Analyses of students' responses to the open-ended question, "Right now in your life, what causes you the most stress?" confirm that academics and schoolwork are major stressors for these youth. Other high-frequency answers included the college admissions process, large projects and assignments, and standardized tests. Students highlighted these school-related factors as causing more stress than other life stressors, such as social issues or family life. Answers such as "family pressure," "divorce," and "parent/sibling illness" did not fall into the top 10 most frequent answers at any school.

Students' responses demonstrated that many feel that schoolwork dominates their day. Certainly, a large share of their time is spent in school, but the demands do not let up after the last bell rings. On average, students in our study reported spending 3.07 hours on homework each night. This does not include time spent online on social activities, such as chatting with friends, or browsing the Internet. One student explained:

> For some reason all teachers love to assign huge amounts of homework on the same nights, which keeps me awake till all hours trying to find the best possible answers because there is a lot of pressure put on us kids to do so well.

Another lamented, "It is not necessarily the difficulty of the work, but the workload itself that causes me the most stress, since the average is about 4–5 hours a night."

On average, these students also spend another two hours each weeknight on extracurricular activities, not including time spent commuting to and from these activities. More than a quarter (28 percent) reported six or more hours of after-school commitments, including homework, each night. These busy schedules leave little room for downtime and rest. In fact, 60.9 percent of the students said that schoolwork or homework frequently keeps them from other things, such as spending time with family and friends; a similar percentage (60.3 percent) reported having to drop an activity they enjoy because of schoolwork and other demands.

While reflecting on their busy schedules and the sources of their stress, several students commented that the pressure is compromising their intellectual development. One student explained:

> I'm stressed because I have so many pointless, mundane assignments that take up large amounts of time, without actually [resulting in] learning anything in class. I don't mind working if I'm actually learning something. I hate wasting my valuable time on assignments that don't accomplish anything for teachers and classes that don't respect me as an intellectual.

Many [students] admitted to copying homework and cheating on tests and quizzes because of the pressure.

Another student wrote,

> If teachers stopped giving out busy work, I'd be able to focus more on important assignments. I always get burnt out when I have to spend a lot of time on useless work.

These students have high grade point averages, but they are frustrated by tedious assignments that hold little meaning for them. Many admitted to copying homework and cheating on tests and quizzes because of the pressure. A full 95 percent of the 11th and 12th grade students in our sample reported that they had cheated at least one time. Even when the work is meaningful, the excessive workload, combined with a busy schedule of outside activities, becomes too much for many of these kids to handle.

Academic Stress Affects Student Well-Being

The stress these students feel not only compromises their learning experience, but also takes a toll on their health and well-being. Given the amount of time they spend completing homework, studying, and pursuing extracurricular activities, it is no wonder that the majority of students in our study reported sleeping fewer hours per night than the 9.25 hours experts suggest they need.

On average, the respondents reported getting 6.8 hours of sleep each weeknight. Over one-third (34.6 percent) reported six or fewer hours of sleep each night. Two-thirds indicated that homework or schoolwork often or always keep them from sleeping. Fifty-four percent reported difficulty sleeping, 56 percent reported experiencing exhaustion as a result of academic stress, and quite a few students listed "not getting enough sleep" as a stressor in and of itself. These students' comments reflect the extent of their sleep deprivation:

- "There are times I do schoolwork from 3 p.m. to 3 a.m. even when I don't procrastinate."

- "I just want more time to sleep and maintain a healthy lifestyle, but school keeps inundating me with work and tests at such a fast and constant rate that I'm always tired and stressed."

- "Just this week I had three all-nighters in a row."

In addition to exhaustion, students attributed other physical symptoms, including headaches and stomach problems, to academic stress. Although 19 percent reported experiencing no physical symptoms in the past month due to academic stress, 44 percent reported experiencing three or more physical symptoms in one month alone. For these youth, it becomes hard to maintain the argument that stress can be healthy.

Stress also adversely affects some students' mental health. Nearly one-quarter of the respondents (24 percent) indicated that they frequently felt depressed in the last month, and 252 students (7 percent) had cut themselves during the same time period.

Some students turn to stimulants to boost their performance. Twenty-four percent of respondents reported that they had used stimulants such as caffeine or over-the-counter alertness pills to help them stay up to study in the last month, and another 274 students (8 percent) reported using illegal stimulants or prescription drugs for the same reason. Other research indicates that these numbers rise dramatically once students enter college.

Students' comments revealed the extent to which some of them are suffering:

- "I get emotionally stressed and have breakdowns, or I go the completely opposite way and stop caring. I wish the administrators would take initiative. I cry all the time!"

- "I was in therapy for anxiety issues last year ... depression from extreme homework and expectations of my coach."

- "I am stressed to the point of developing chronic insomnia."

- "When I feel especially stressed out, I feel like intoxication is the best way out."

Clearly, these students are experiencing distress. Their grades may indicate that they are meeting or exceeding academic standards, but their words indicate that they are sacrificing their health and well-being.

Schools Are Responding to Student Problems

The schools that participated in this study joined a research-based intervention program known as Challenge Success. This program, based at the Stanford University School of Education, guides school teams of multiple stakeholders as they design and implement site-based policies and practices that reduce student stress and promote greater student engagement, academic integrity, health, and well-being.

Soon after joining the program, these schools administered a baseline survey to a representative sample of their student bodies to determine the extent to which their students experienced academic stress and to examine links among physical and mental health, student motivation, and achievement. The survey data help participating schools not only identify specific problem areas, but also generate community-wide understanding of these problems.

After developing this shared understanding, schools implemented a variety of strategies to reduce student stress and increase well-being. Most schools created more opportunities for students to receive support from staff, developed test and project calendars to help ease students' workload, and revised homework policies. Some also modified college counseling practices, reformed the grading system or grading policies, and created honor codes or new academic integrity policies.

These are the strategies that schools found most helpful:

- Changes to the schedule: Allowing fewer transitions and more downtime or free periods, adding more tutorial time or advisory periods, or going to a block or modified block schedule.

- Staff training and development: Conducting workshops on engagement and alternative assessments.

- Altering exams: Reducing their weight, moving them to before winter break, increasing time between exams, and replacing exams with projects.

At a school where the daily bell schedule and the exam schedule were significantly modified, students reported experiencing less stress. The vast majority of 10th and 11th graders (86 percent and 83 percent, respectively) agreed that adding free periods to the schedule, lengthening the class periods and advisories, and reducing the number of classes each day had effectively eased their workload. More than three-quarters of these sophomores and juniors (77 percent and 76 percent respectively) agreed that rescheduling exams from after the winter break to before the break reduced their stress. Administrators attested to the positive effects of the reforms and commented that student grades, test scores, and college admissions all stayed high, but the stress decreased.

Even seemingly modest reform efforts had positive effects. At another participating school, for instance, some advanced placement (AP) teachers worked to decrease student stress and increase student engagement with learning. One AP Biology teacher cut the homework load in half, eliminated summer work, and encouraged frequent dialogue with students and parents about student well-being. For two years in a row, the AP Biology test scores in his class have gone up, and students have reported higher levels of engagement with the material and less stress. An AP Calculus teacher at another school had similar success when he reduced homework and cut back on the number of problems he had students do each night.

His students did less homework than students in other high-level math classes, but they scored as well on the AP exams—with a lot less stress.

Schools can achieve positive results without the undue pressures.

Intervention Program Encourages Collaborative Solution

In response to the overwhelming workload at her school, one student made this plea:

> Don't push students farther than their limit. All my teachers say, "I'm treating you like this because that's how you'll be treated in college." Guess what? I'm not in college; I'm 15 and in high school *for a reason.*

This student is right. The physical and mental health tolls we've depicted are not appropriate for any youth, and educators and parents need to be aware of the problem and attuned to the signs of student stress.

The Challenge Success program is not advocating that teachers water down their curriculums or eliminate homework or even abolish tests and exams. But we see the negative ramifications of a system that pushes students too far, and we know that schools can achieve positive results without the undue pressures.

To be fair, the schools are not the sole source of this problem—parents, students, federal policies, and colleges and universities all play a role. Because the problem is multifaceted, we encourage multiple stakeholders—teachers, students, parents, counselors, and administrators—to work together to formulate plans for change. When everyone recognizes the need for change and has a say in the reform process, schools can indeed foster healthier environments in which student learning and student well-being are mutually reinforcing.

4

Academic Pressure Is Not as Dire as Claimed

Jay Mathews

Jay Mathews is an education columnist for The Washington Post. *He has written several books on education, including* Work Hard. Be Nice.: How Two Inspired Teachers Created the Most Promising School in America.

The documentary film Race to Nowhere: The Dark Side of America's Achievement Culture *has been shown to groups of educators and families across the country. The film seems to rely more on feeling than fact when declaring that students in the United States are drowning under the pressure of large amounts of homework. Data based on time diaries collected by at least two prominent higher education research groups refute this claim, showing that instead students are in reality spending far less time studying than on leisure activities. The demands of excess homework may be true in some isolated incidences especially related to students who are taking Advanced Placement courses in high school, but it is definitely not a 'silent epidemic' as the film's producer claims.*

Vicki Abeles's film *Race to Nowhere: The Dark Side of America's Achievement Culture* may be the most popular documentary in the United States without a theater distribution deal. Parents and students have flocked to more than 1,700 screenings in 47 states and 20 countries.

It is a well-intended project that raises a vital issue: harmful academic pressure on students in some college-conscious homes. Then the film goes haywire by suggesting that too much homework is a national problem, when the truth is that high school students, on average, are doing too little.

Abeles has spunk. She agreed to an e-mail discussion and did not waver when I challenged her notion that all teenagers, not just the most affluent 10 percent, are drowning in textbooks and term papers.

I cited time diaries collected by the University of Michigan Institute for Social Research showing that 15- to 17-year-olds in 2002 and 2003 devoted about 3 1/2 hours a day to TV and leisure. Their average time spent studying was 42 minutes. I pointed out that the UCLA [University of California Los Angeles] Higher Education Research Institute survey of college freshmen shows that about two-thirds did an hour or less of homework a night in high school.

Abeles replied: "The University of Michigan study you reference actually shows that the amount of homework assigned to kids age 6 to 9 almost tripled in the 1990s." That's true but misleading. Daily homework for 6- to 8-year-olds increased, on average, from 8 minutes in 1981 to 22 in 2003. Even when tripled, that homework took less time than watching an episode of *Hannah Montana Forever*. (For the record, I'm dubious about the value of homework in elementary grades.)

The UCLA Higher Education Research Institute survey of college freshmen shows that about two-thirds did an hour or less of homework a night in high school.

Test Scores Remain Stagnant

Abeles and her film focus not on data but feelings, which are important, but some of us yearn for more. She prefers to cite "our experience at screenings" as proof that we suffer from a "silent epidemic" of "pressure-cooker education," and not just in places such as McLean [Virginia] and Beverly Hills [California]. But she doesn't explain why average American teens—if they are really being dragooned into heavy studying—have shown no significant gains in reading or math over the past three decades.

She and her film blame Advanced Placement [AP] courses for some of the pressure. She tells interviewers that she has heard that some suburban schools are dropping AP, when, in fact, the program is growing and even altering courses to give students more of the depth and choice Abeles says they need.

Some students and families overdo AP. Abeles is right to point that out. But AP, like the college pressure that concerns her, is concentrated in only a few places. My annual Challenge Index rankings, moving this year from *Newsweek* to washingtonpost.com, show that only 7 percent of high schools have AP participation rates higher than what would be achieved with half of juniors and half of seniors taking just one AP course and test a year. Most high schools do far less.

Abeles says low-income students suffer from pressure because of a narrow focus on testing and lessons that are irrelevant to their lives. The urban high school teachers I know go to great lengths to be relevant and wish more students would worry about exams. But, like most American teens, they can get by without doing much, and so they do just that.

5

America's Achievement Culture Harms the Education System

Jim Taylor

Jim Taylor is recognized for his work in the psychology of performance in business, parenting, and sports. He is the author of twelve books and is a frequent blogger on his own website as well as other sites, including psychologytoday.com, fastcompany .com, and sfgate.com.

The documentary film titled Race to Nowhere *examines the high-pressure world of academic achievement many students are entwined in today and should serve as a wake-up call to parents, teachers, and school administrators. There are many factors that have caused the US educational system to kick into overdrive. A depressed economy has left many families feeling vulnerable about their futures. The No Child Left Behind Act of 2001 has placed an increased emphasis on standardized test scores in assessing the performance of both students and teachers. Schools have responded by expanding the amount of homework for students with the hope that doing so will improve test scores, even in the face of evidence showing this approach does little to enhance achievement. With an amplified attention on testing, students may be missing out on such higher order skills as critical thinking and creativity that they will need to succeed in college and beyond.*

R ace to the Top is the name given to President [Barack] Obama's education-reform program that is supposed to change the education system in America. But what it should be called is *Race to Nowhere*, which happens to be the name of a powerful new documentary by Vicki Abeles that explores, as the film's subtitle states, the dark side of America's achievement culture.

I saw *Race to Nowhere* recently with my wife and was blown away by its message. As the father of two young girls, it scared the heck out of me what lies ahead for them. And as the author of two parenting books with similar messages as the film, it was a real reminder of the very human and societal costs of our current education system. Through interviews with students, parents, teachers, and other educators, and bookended by a story about a 13-year-old girl who committed suicide after failing a math test, we see the price that so many young people are paying for trying to hang onto the runaway train of academic overachievement.

The pressure young people are under to achieve that elusive notion of success has become, for many, a crippling weight on their shoulders and the price tag is high. *Race to Nowhere* presents some compelling arguments against the emphasis on test scores that increased exponentially with the passage of the federal No Child Left Behind Act [NCLB] (it should be called the Almost Every Child Left Behind Act, given its abysmal record in raising test scores or graduation rates, much less actually educating children). Students now focus on memorizing facts (and then forget them shortly after), find learning to be aversive rather than inspiring, and see no problem with cheating to get ahead (in the 1940s, 20% of students admitted to cheating in high school; today, well over 75% make the same admission).

Student Well-Being Suffers

The physical and psychological toll is heavy as well. Students rate academic stress as their greatest source of stress, exceeding family problems and bullying. Rates of stress-related illness, depression, anxiety, and burnout are on the rise. Academic-performance-enhancing drugs, such as the ADHD [Attention Deficit Hyperactivity Disorder] drug Adderall to enhance energy and focus and beta blockers to reduce anxiety, are SOP (Standard Operating Procedure) on high-school and college campuses. And teenage suicide rates, particularly among teenage girls, have increased dramatically in recent years.

What is this culture of faux achievement like? Let's look at more statistics from the film. More than 70% of young people don't get the recommended amount of sleep for their stage of development (and sleep is essential for healthy brain development). Children have lost 12 hours of free time each week while homework time has increased by 50%. Homework is now given as early as first grade and reaches its apogee in high school where students now spend up to seven hours a night on homework, despite evidence demonstrating that it has no value up to 5th grade and loses its value if greater than one hour for middle-school students and two hours for high-school students. And talk about being unprepared; 40% of students require remedial classes when they get to college.

> *The child-development, tutoring, and testing industries are an almost $10 billion scam that feeds on the fears of parents that their children will be left behind.*

The numbers are truly frightening, but the interviews of students, parents, and teachers in *Race to Nowhere* really hit home. The frustration among teachers, the sadness among students, and the fear and pain felt by parents bring the cold, hard data to life. No parent can leave the film without a profound feeling of disgust at our education system, a mama or papa bear's instinct to protect their cubs, a determination to catalyze a transformation, and, sadly, a feeling of futility about changing such an inertial system.

A Culture Driven by Fear

How did this pressure-cooker of an achievement culture (and, by the way, it can be found in sports and the arts as well as in school) develop? There are many culprits, some legitimate and others manufactured and dishonest. The economic instability and uncertainty that has increased in recent years has created genuine fear among parents for their children's future. This fear drives parents to push their children relentlessly to ensure that they get ahead in school. Popular culture, and the aspirational dreams it has spawned, has redefined the meaning of success upward in terms of wealth, status, and materialism, so that being merely competent at one's job and comfortable in one's lifestyle is akin to failure; everything must be bigger and better and more, more, more. The availability and demand for a college education, particularly in the "best" schools (read Ivy League or its equivalent), have far outpaced supply, so competition is greater than ever (I attended Middlebury College back in the day, but I probably couldn't get accepted now with my GPA [grade point average] and SAT scores). The child-development, tutoring, and testing industries are an almost $10 billion scam that feeds on the fears of parents that their children will be left behind.

Today's students may lack the critical thinking, creativity, and focus necessary to survive, much less thrive, as they enter higher education and the working world.

The ramifications for the students themselves extend beyond the current physical and psychological toll; there may very well be a price they pay in their futures. For example, such a mind- and body-numbing educational experience will suck any joy of learning they may have right out of them. The current emphasis on rote memorization will sap their internal motivation to learn. As highlighted in *Race to Nowhere*, today's students may lack the critical thinking, creativity, and focus necessary to survive, much less thrive, as they enter higher education and the working world.

Educational Reform Is Slow to Be Enacted

The toll on our country may be equally dramatic. Are we leaving this generation's young people ill prepared to assume the mantle of leadership? Will they have the knowledge and tools necessary to continue America's arc as the frontrunner in innovation and progress? The low rankings currently held by our students compared to other countries on international achievement tests don't bode well for their or our future.

Is there hope? I'm not optimistic that effective federal or even state education reform will ever happen given the political hot potato that it is. But there appears to be a smidgen of hope at other points in the educational food chain. Colleges and universities, one of the big culprits of this academic arms race, have the power to ratchet down the pressure and some appear to be getting the message. A growing number of prominent schools are not accepting AP [Advanced Placement] courses or are making SAT scores optional. Some high schools are following this lead by abolishing AP classes from their curricula (with, by the way, no damage to college acceptances).

6

Global Homework Practices Do Not Always Correlate with Performance

Penn State Live

Penn State Live is the official online news source for Pennsylvania State University.

Available international data indicate that there is no clear-cut evidence that increased homework leads to improved test scores. The impact of homework depends largely on the caliber of a country's educational program and attitudes within that country toward homework. Although discussions continue as to how best to raise achievement levels, governments and political groups would be wise to avoid creating blanket policies that could potentially do more harm than good.

A study of global homework patterns suggests that the benefits of more homework assignments to boost student test scores may vary widely according to the grade level, the quality of a nation's schools and the perceived value of homework. Therefore, researchers caution that government and education policymakers need to consider the appropriate grade levels and related impact before trying to create overall homework policies for schools.

"Over the past two decades, much of the policy discussion in the U.S. has focused on increasing national test scores to the level of international standards," says Gerald LeTendre, professor of education policy studies at Penn State [University] and lead author of the study. "More standardized testing drives educators to give more homework in order to prepare for these exams. Homework has moved to center stage in the debate over how nations can improve their economic competitiveness by boosting student scores. Yet, national policies aimed at simply increasing homework amounts are unlikely to produce increases in average student achievement scores."

For U.S. schools, the study shows a negative relationship between higher homework amounts and student achievement in elementary schools, and only a very small benefit in middle schools.

Comparisons Are Difficult

Overall, the data show that U.S. students receive an average amount of daily homework, compared with other nations. But the percentage of U.S. elementary students with four or more hours per night has risen to 8 percent, well above the 1 percent reported in Japan and 5 percent in Taiwan, two countries considered benchmarks for U.S. students. Five percent of the U.S. middle school students in the survey reported four or more hours of homework per night, compared to 3 percent in Taiwan and 1 percent in Japan.

LeTendre, professor of education policy studies, and Motoko Akiba, University of Missouri, Columbia, analyzed data from the Third International Math and Science Survey (TIMSS) for 1995 and 2003, selecting 18 nations to examine overall trends. They presented their findings today [February 27, 2007] at the annual Comparative and International Education Society [conference] in Baltimore, Md.

"An overlooked factor is the quality of the education in a nation's public schools," the researchers say. "Some developing nations with fewer resources may see an increase in student achievement with more homework because the homework helps student to catch up in their skills. Students in schools of well-funded nations may not need to spend as much time on homework."

For U.S. schools, the study shows a negative relationship between higher homework amounts and student achievement in elementary schools, and only a very small benefit in middle schools. At the middle school level, the students who did some homework, but not excessive amounts, seem to score the best. The U.S. falls into the "balanced" pattern of homework completion found in many nations where students who do modest amounts of homework (30 minutes to an hour an a half per night) have higher test scores than peers who do no homework or those who study more than four hours per night.

"We may need to know more about the specific relationship between national policies or practices related to homework," the researchers add. "The role of homework in a child's life and a nation's educational policies has been hotly debated, and there is now a significant backlash in the U.S. against homework."

7

The Value of Homework Needs Further Research

Alfie Kohn

Alfie Kohn writes and speaks extensively on human behavior, education, and parenting. He is the author of twelve books, including Feel-Bad Education: And Other Contrarian Essays on Children and Schooling. *Kohn has been featured on numerous TV and radio programs, including* The Today Show *and* Oprah.

At first glance, research results seem to support traditional methods in education, but follow-up studies that involve looking at data across a longer period of time often refute the results of the initial findings. A case in point is found in studies on homework. The research that is for a brief period of time does show that homework proves beneficial in increasing student achievement. However, more in-depth analysis indicates that longer studies show that homework has a much smaller impact than revealed in studies of a shorter duration. A healthy skepticism is required to understand the real meaning hidden behind the headlines.

It's not unusual to read that a new study has failed to replicate—or has even reversed—the findings of an earlier study. The effect can be disconcerting, particularly when medical research announces that what was supposed to be good for us turns out to be dangerous, or vice versa.

Qualifications and reversals also show up in investigations of education and human behavior, but here an interesting pattern seems to emerge. At first a study seems to validate traditional practices, but then subsequent studies—those that follow subjects for longer periods of time or use more sophisticated outcome measures—call that result into question.

That's not really surprising when you stop to think about it. Traditional practices (with respect to teaching students but also to raising children and managing employees) often consist of what might be called a "doing to"—as opposed to a "working with"—approach, the point being to act on people to achieve a specific goal. These strategies sometimes succeed in producing an effect in the short term. Research—which itself is often limited in duration or design—may certify the effort as successful. But when you watch what happens later on, or you look more carefully at the impact of these interventions, the initial findings have a way of going up in smoke.

Consider three such traditional practices: using rewards to change people's behavior, making students do additional academic assignments after they get home from school, and teaching by means of old-fashioned telling (sometimes known as direct instruction). What happens in each case when you look at short-term results, and what happens when you then extend the length of the study?

The longer you track the kids, the more likely that a drill-and-skill approach will show no benefits and may even appear to be harmful.

Results Vary with Study Length

1. An ambitious investigation of various types of preschools looked specifically at children from low-income families in Illinois. The two educational approaches that produced the greatest impact on achievement in reading and arithmetic were both highly structured, one of them a behaviorist technique called Direct Instruction (or DISTAR) that emphasizes the use of scripted drill in academic skills and praise for correct responses.

Most studies would have left it at that, and the press doubtless would have published the findings, which suggests that this model is superior to more child-centered preschools. (Take that, you progressives!) Luckily, though, this particular group of researchers had both the funding and the interest to continue tracking the children long after they left preschool. And it turned out that with each year that went by, the advantage of two years of regimented reading-skills instruction evaporated, soon proving equivalent—in terms of effects on test scores—to "an intensive 1-hour reading readiness support program" that had been provided to another group. "This follow-up data lends little support for the introduction of formal reading instruction during the preschool years for children from low-income homes," the researchers wrote.[1]

One difference did show up much later, however: Almost three quarters of the kids in play-oriented and Montessori preschools ended up graduating from high school, as compared to less than half of the direct-instruction kids, which was about the same rate for those who hadn't attended preschool at all. (Other longitudinal studies of preschool have found similar results: The longer you track the kids, the more likely that a drill-and-skill approach will show no benefits and may even appear to be harmful.)

2. For various reasons that I've reviewed elsewhere there's reason to doubt that requiring children to do homework has any meaningful academic benefit. In elementary school in particular, there isn't even a *correlation* between doing homework (vs. doing none) or doing more homework (vs. doing less), on the one hand, and any measures of achievement—even such conventional (and, I believe, dubious) measures as grades or standardized test scores. But one prominent researcher—who does place stock in these measures—noticed something inter-

esting when he reviewed 48 comparisons in 17 published reports of research projects that had lasted anywhere from two to thirty weeks: The longer the duration of the study, the less impact that homework had.[2]

This researcher speculated that less homework may have been assigned during any given week in the longer-lasting studies, but he offered no evidence that this was true. So here's another theory: The studies finding the greatest effect were those that captured less of what goes on in the real world by virtue of being so brief. View a small, unrepresentative slice of a child's life and it may appear that homework makes a contribution to school achievement; keep watching and that contribution is eventually revealed to be illusory.

There's reason to doubt that requiring children to do homework has any meaningful academic benefit.

---

3. Many people who are concerned with promoting healthy lifestyles assume that it makes sense to offer an incentive for losing weight, quitting smoking, or going to the gym. The only real question on this view is how to manage the details of the reward program. In an experiment published in 2008, people who received either of two types of incentives lost more weight after about four months than did those in the control group. (Unfortunately, there was no non-incentive weight-loss program; subjects got either money or no help at all.) At the seven-month mark, however, the effect melted away even if the pounds didn't. There was no statistically significant weight difference between those in either of the incentive conditions and those who received nothing. This result, by the way, is typical of what just about all studies of weight loss and smoking cessation have found: The longer you look, the less chance that rewards will do any good—and they may actually do harm.[3]

4. Belief in the value of rewards is, if anything, even stronger in the corporate world, where it's widely believed—indeed, taken on faith—that dangling financial incentives in front of employees will cause them to work harder. Conversely, if workers are provided with such an incentive and it's then removed, their productivity would be expected to decline. An unusual occurrence in a manufacturing company provided a real-world opportunity to test this assumption: A new collective bargaining agreement for a group of welders resulted in the sudden elimination of a long-standing incentive plan. The immediate result was that production did indeed drop. But as with the preschool study, this researcher decided to continue tracking the company records—and discovered that, in the absence of rewards, the welders' production soon began to rise and eventually reached a level as high or higher than it had been before.[4]

5. Sometimes a different result emerges when a new study is done better as opposed to merely lasting longer. The topic of homework provides a striking example. One of the most frequently cited investigations in the field was published in the early 1980s by a researcher named Timothy Keith, who looked at survey results from tens of thousands of high school students and concluded that homework had a positive relationship to achievement, at least at that age. But ten years later, he and a colleague took a closer look—this time considering homework alongside other possible influences on learning such as quality of instruction, motivation, and which classes the students took. When all these variables were entered into the equation simultaneously, the result was "puzzling and surprising": Homework no longer had any meaningful effect on achievement at all, even in high school.[5]

6. Finally, what happens when a second researcher comes along and does a study that's both longer *and* better than the original? Consider a report published in 2004 that showed third and fourth graders who received "an extreme type of di-

rect instruction [in a science unit] in which the goals, the materials, the examples, the explanations, and the pace of instruction [were] all teacher controlled" did better than their classmates who were allowed to design their own procedures. Frankly, the way they had set up the latter condition wasn't representative of the strategies most experts recommend for promoting discovery and exploration. Nevertheless, the finding may have given pause to progressive educators—at least in the context of elementary school science teaching.

Or, rather, it may have given them pause for three years. That's how much time passed before another study was published that investigated the same issue in the same discipline for kids of the same age. The two differences: the second study looked at the effects six months later instead of only one week later; and the second study used a more sophisticated type of assessment of the students' learning. Sure enough, it turned out that any advantage of direct instruction disappeared over time. And on one of the measures, pure exploration not only proved more impressive than direct instruction but also more impressive than a combination of the two—which suggests that direct instruction can be not merely ineffective but positively counterproductive.[6]

Despite their diversity, these six sets of studies hardly exhaust the universe of research that forces a reevaluation of what came before. Still, any observer willing to connect the dots may end up not only waiting for replications to be performed before accepting any preliminary conclusion—a reasonable posture in general—but more skeptical of studies that seem to support traditional practices in particular.

Notes

1. Merle B. Karnes, Allan M. Shwedel, and Mark B. Williams, "A Comparison of Five Approaches for Educating Young Children from Low-Income Homes." In *As the Twig Is Bent . . . : Lasting Effects of Preschool Programs,* ed.

by the Consortium for Longitudinal Studies (Hillsdale, N.J.: Erlbaum, 1983). For a summary of other research on early-childhood education, see www.alfiekohn.org/teaching/ece.htm.

2. Harris Cooper, *The Battle Over Homework*. 2nd ed. Thousand Oaks, CA: Corwin, 2001, p. 16.

3. Kevin G. Volpp et al., "Financial Incentive-Based Approaches for Weight Loss," *Journal of the American Medical Association*, 300 (December 10, 2008): 2631–37. For a review of other research on the (lack of long-term) effects of financial incentives on weight loss and smoking cessation, see www.alfiekohn.org/miscellaneous/healthresearch.htm. That review also appears in Alfie Kohn, *Feel-Bad Education . . . And Other Contrarian Essays on Children and Schooling* (Boston: Beacon Press, 2011), pp. 199–204.

4. Harold F. Rothe, "Output Rates Among Welders: Productivity and Consistency Following Removal of a Financial Incentive System," *Journal of Applied Psychology* 54 (1970): 549–51.

5. Valerie A. Cool and Timothy Z. Keith, "Testing a Model of School Learning: Direct and Indirect Effects on Academic Achievement," *Contemporary Educational Psychology* 16 (1991): 28–44.

6. The original study: David Klahr and Milena Nigam, "The Equivalence of Learning Paths in Early Science Instruction: Effects of Direct Instruction and Discovery Learning," *Psychological Science* 15 (2004): 661–67. The newer study: David Dean, Jr. and Deanna Kuhn, "Direct Instruction vs. Discovery: The Long View," *Science Education* 91 (2007): 384–97.

8

Student Performance Suffers When Homework Is Optional

Susan Graham

Susan Graham has taught family and consumer science for twenty-five years. She is a national board certified teacher, a former regional Virginia teacher of the year, and a fellow of the Teacher Leaders Network.

The school district in Irving, Texas, stopped counting homework assignments as part of a student's grades beginning with the 2010–2011 school year. The results of this experiment proved interesting in the ongoing battles over the necessity and value of homework. After six weeks, over half of the high school students were failing a class—a much higher percentage than the previous year. Based on the data from Irving, high school students seem to lack the judgment and experience necessary to know on their own when additional studying or outside class work is needed in order to pass tests and complete projects. Just as sports teams understand that conditioning and drills before games are vital to success, maybe the practice homework affords is indeed a necessary part of mastering a subject.

We've been working hard at 21st Century Learning for a decade now. We're *setting new paradigms for learning* and "creating virtual learning communities" that are "responsive to the needs of all students" by providing "on demand asynchronous instruction" that is "paced by student readiness." That's great, but down in Irving, Texas, *they are slugging it out over homework*. Because, the *Dallas Morning News* writes,

> At the beginning of the school year, Irving stopped counting homework toward grades, but tests, essays, projects and performances were counted.

> And guess what . . .

> After the first six weeks of the year, about half of all the district's high school students—4,597—were failing one or more classes, compared with 3,412 students who were during the same period last year.

It seems that the average 15-year-old cannot make precise judgments about whether they need practice and/or opportunities for application of concepts to be fully prepared to demonstrate mastery. But not to worry; that's been addressed because

> Teachers also must allow students who fail an exam to retest and give other students the option to do so if they want to improve their grade, even if they were caught cheating.

Now granted, you can't make anything higher than a 90 if you retake a test and it's not clear that if you made 50 the first time, and cheated the second time and made 60, whether you could then have a third try. Can you strike out completely? Not clear. So why no homework?

> The district initially stopped counting homework because administrators felt it didn't measure students' actual learning as much as other assessments.

Why not? Does that mean the homework was not meaningful? Does it mean the students cheated and so the work they turned in did not reflect their understanding? Does it mean that the students simply did not attempt homework, got zeros and then failed? Can't projects, essays, performance, and research be homework? And really, isn't conjugating five Latin verbs or completing five calculus problems a performance? Sure, a "no homework" policy makes life easier for everyone. The kids can opt out of assignments they consider unproductive. Parents don't have to nag. Teachers don't have to grade. It ought to be the ultimate win/win/win!

> But parents and teachers were troubled that students appeared less prepared for tests because they weren't completing their work. They also were concerned that students who were poor test takers would fall behind.

Benefits of Homework Show Up in Its Absence

Maybe parents and teachers realize that expecting a teenager to self-assess their learning exceeds the expertise and the maturity of most 15-year-olds. If parents and teachers are life and academic coaches for adolescents, maybe there are lessons to be learned from coaches in professional sports. Every season we hear about athletes who are penalized for deciding to skip preseason practice because they have determined they don't need it. The funny thing is that although these adults are the best of the best, their coaches have no qualms about setting and enforcing expectations for conditioning, drills and practice. It seems that, no matter how good you are at something, practice helps and that most of us could use some outside motivation to get that practice accomplished.

> The changes come because school districts are required to adopt grading policies as the result of a state law enacted last year [2009]. The law barred districts from setting minimum grades for students. For example, some districts previously did not allow teachers to assign report card grades lower than a 50. Now they can. The law also said students may be given an opportunity to redo class work or tests that they fail.

And so, here we stand—a decade into the 21st Century—and we're still fighting the homework wars. Are adolescents noble savages who are constrained by false constructs such as homework? Or are they insufficiently trained workers who need to learn to conform to consistent workplace expectations? Will more homework ensure that we leave no child behind, as well-intended but uninformed stakeholders continue to race willy-nilly to the top of the statehouse steps, legislating what "sounds like a good idea in theory" into education policy?

It seems that, no matter how good you are at something, practice helps and that most of us could use some outside motivation to get that practice accomplished.

I'm not picking on Irving—the grading conundrum is real. . . . It's just interesting to me that as we begin to explore reinventing school in theory, there is still an awful lot of energy and passion expended on how much homework there should be, whether to give zeros, and whether weighted or total point grading systems are best, how many grades should be collected per week, and what to do about late work.

In a perfect world, everyone would be intrinsically motivated to enrich their minds and produce their best efforts. It's not a perfect world. But when high school grading policy begins to be legislated at a state or national level, I wonder how we can ever move toward substantive changes in policy. Good intentions? Maybe. Good publicity? Probably. Good policy? I don't think so.

9

Parents Should Take Action Against Excessive Homework

Nancy Kalish

Nancy Kalish is coauthor of The Case Against Homework: How Homework Is Hurting Children and What Parents Can Do About It *and writes frequently about education issues. She is a former senior editor at* Child *magazine and has also been a monthly columnist for* Redbook *and* Working Mother. *Kalish has appeared on* The Today Show, CBS Evening News, *and* ABC Eyewitness News.

More parents are fighting back against the homework status quo in an attempt to reclaim family time. Even parents who previously had embraced the tradition of homework are finding that as their children advance through the grades, too much homework is proving more detrimental than helpful. Many schools are listening and adjusting homework policies to eliminate weekend and holiday homework and limiting the amounts given on other days. Teachers report that giving less homework means they have less grading to do, which allows them more time to plan engaging and creative lessons.

I used to be extremely pro-homework. In fact, I once wrote an article for this very magazine [*Parenting*] telling readers how to get kids to stop whining and knuckle down to work. Back then, I could afford to be smug: My second-grader was happily zooming through her ten minutes a night. But a few years later, Allison started coming home with four hours of homework each night, and everything changed. Now there was not only whining but also begging, yelling, and crying—sometimes from both of us. The worst part: hearing my previously enthusiastic learner repeatedly swear how much she hated school.

I'd always assumed homework was essential. But when I finally looked into the research about it, I was floored to find there's little to support homework—especially in vast quantities. While not every child gets too much, many kids are now overloaded as early as kindergarten. I was appalled (I even cowrote a book about it, *The Case Against Homework*), so you can bet that this time around, you won't be getting any "how to be a good homework cop" tips from me.

Instead, I'm here to call you to action. You can change things for your child—even for the whole school. There are more and more frustrated parents and wised-up schools around the country, so why should your child keep suffering through hours of work? A less-homework revolution is brewing, and you can join it.

A less-homework revolution is brewing, and you can join it.

Parental Pushback Can Lessen the Homework Load

Like me, Christine Hendricks, a mother of three in Glenrock, WY, had always believed in homework. Then her daughter, Maddie, entered elementary school. "By the fourth grade, she had so much, there was no time for after-school activities, playing, or simply enjoying our evenings together. We were always stressed, and I knew many other families were also miserable." Hendricks decided things had to change—and she had a unique advantage: She's the principal of Glenrock's Grant

Elementary School. Together with her teachers, she looked into the research and found what I did: Homework's not what it's cracked up to be. "We decided to do an experiment and eliminate most homework," she says. The one exception: occasional studying for a test. "This is only our second year without it, but there have been no backslides in the classroom or in test scores," says Hendricks. "Parents say their kids enjoy reading again because there's no pressure. In fact, there have been no negative effects whatsoever. And there's much less stress at our house, too." We're not all in a position to fast-track a solution as Hendricks did, but we still have power.

In Toronto [Canada], Frank Bruni decided to do something when a pediatrician told him that his 13-year-old son should exercise more. Says Bruni, "I thought to myself, 'And when would he do that?'" So Bruni organized other parents and lobbied the Toronto School District to hold public meetings, presenting the research behind homework. The result is a new policy that affects more than 300,000 kids, limiting homework to reading in elementary school, eliminating holiday homework, and stating the value of family time. Canada's education minister now wants all the country's school boards to make sure students aren't being overloaded. "It's so gratifying to know that this year, Toronto's kids are going to have a life," says Bruni. "It shows you just how much parents can do when they try."

Homework is such an established part of education, it's hard to believe it's not all that beneficial, especially in large quantities. But the truth is, a recent Duke University review of numerous studies found almost no correlation between homework and long-term achievement in elementary school, and only a moderate correlation in middle school. "More is not better," says Harris Cooper, Ph.D., a professor of psychology and neuroscience who conducted the review. In fact, according to guidelines endorsed by the National Education Association, teachers should assign no more than ten minutes per grade level per night (that's ten minutes total for a first-grader, 30 minutes for a third-grader).

More Homework Does Not Lead to Higher Achievement

Pile on more and it can backfire. "Most kids are simply developmentally unable to sit and learn for longer," says Cooper. Remember: Many have already been glued to their desks for seven hours, especially at schools that have cut gym, recess, art, and music to cram in more instructional time. If you add on two hours of homework each night, these children are working a 45-hour week. Some argue that we need to toughen kids up for high school, college, and the workforce. But there are other ways to teach responsibility, such as the chores that parents often have to let slide because of studying. And too much homework is actually sapping our children's strength, natural curiosity, and love of learning. "Kids are developing more school-related stomachaches, headaches, sleep problems, and depression than ever before," says William Crain, Ph.D., a professor of psychology at the City College of New York and author of *Reclaiming Childhood: Letting Children Be Children in Our Achievement-Oriented Society.* "We're seeing kids who are burned out by fourth grade. Soon, it will be by second grade." Too much homework also means that kids miss out on active playtime, essential for learning social skills, proper brain development, and warding off childhood obesity.

All this work doesn't even make educational sense. "It's counterintuitive, but more practice or the wrong kind of practice doesn't necessarily make perfect," says Kylene Beers, president of the National Council of Teachers of English and author of *When Kids Can't Read, What Teachers Can Do.* For example, children are able to memorize long lists of spelling words—but many will misspell them the following week.

"Instead, they should spend the time reading and writing, and practicing words that are at the appropriate level for each child," says Beers. According to the U.S. Department of Education, most often a math teacher can tell after checking five algebraic equations whether a student has understood the necessary concepts. Even more important, whether it's algebra or addition, five problems is enough to tell if a student doesn't understand a concept. Practicing dozens of homework problems incorrectly only cements the wrong method into his brain. Naturally, some kids need more practice before math skills become automatic, but pages of problems rarely help the whole class. In addition, teachers who assign large numbers of problems are often unable to do anything more than spot-check homework. That means errors are missed—and some children truly are left behind.

Too much homework is actually sapping our children's strength, natural curiosity, and love of learning.

So why are schools ignoring all these guidelines? "Many teachers are under greater pressure than ever before to assign more homework," says Beers. "Some of it comes from parents, some from the administration and the desire for high scores on standardized tests." And here's a surprise: Your child's teachers have probably never taken a course that covers what constitutes good or bad homework, how much to give, and the research behind it. "I'm disappointed to admit that colleges of education simply don't offer specific training in homework," says Beers. Cooper adds, "Teachers are winging it."

Changing the Homework Philosophy

A revolution has to begin somewhere, and as Christine Hendricks, the Wyoming principal and mom, proves, that somewhere isn't only on the coasts or in big cities. It's in communities and schools all over the country.

After teaching math for several years at South Valley Middle School in Liberty, MO, Joel Wazac realized that his students were rarely finishing the reams of problems he sent home. So he and other math teachers decided to eliminate homework and concentrate on making class lessons more engaging. "I had more time for planning when I wasn't grading thousands of problems each night," says Wazac. "And when a student didn't understand something, instead of a parent trying to puzzle it out, I was right there to help him." The result: Grades went up and the school's standardized math test scores are the highest they've ever been.

Many parents are the ones leading the fight against homework overload and winning.

In some cases, entire schools, such as Mason-Rice Elementary in Newton, MA, have limited homework according to the "ten-minute rule." The Raymond Park Middle School in Indianapolis has a written policy instructing teachers to "assign homework only when you feel the assignment is valuable. A night off is better than homework which serves no worthwhile purpose." Others, such as Oak Knoll Elementary in Menlo Park, CA, are eliminating elementary school homework altogether. If these schools can do it, why can't yours?

Many parents are the ones leading the fight against homework overload and winning. In Danville, CA, Kerry Dickinson, a mother of two, spearheaded the effort by organizing more than 100 parents to convince the local school district to revise its homework policy. The policy still exceeds the "ten minutes per grade" rule, but it discourages weekend and holiday homework and stresses the value of family time. "Is it perfect? Not even close," says Dickinson, who has a teaching credential herself. "But it's progress." You may feel more comfortable starting smaller—but that's a great way to get the revolution brewing in your community. Aubrey King is a mom who found that teachers can be more responsive (and sympathetic) than you might think. "Normally, we have no time for after-school activities, the park, or even getting an ice cream cone," says King, the Colorado Springs mother of a third- and a sixth-grader, as well as three younger children. But when one child's homework interfered with the family's preparations for Christmas, it was the last straw. King e-mailed the teacher, who promptly eliminated all assignments for the entire class until after winter break.

Another step in the right direction: Krisi Repp of Gray Summit, MO, sent each of her three children's teachers a letter detailing her family's already busy schedule and gently informing them that homework was interfering with sleep, exercise, dinner, church, and precious time together. "Several teachers commented 'I never thought about that' or 'You're right,'" Repp reports. "Many don't have school-age children yet themselves. They're not going to know any better unless we speak out."

10

Homework Has Value When It Reinforces Learning

Lisa Mangione

Lisa Mangione is a special education teacher at Sweet Home Middle School in Amherst, New York, and a fellow of the Western New York Writing Project.

Student homework endures as a topic of hot debate. Parents, teachers, and students all have points of view. Aside from questions of quantity, homework assignments need to be examined for how effective they are in achieving educational goals for students. Homework should be a form of practice and something students can accomplish without parental support.

By now, I've grown familiar with the prelude. "I have a teacher question for you," my friend asks me on a fairly routine basis. Invariably, there is a parent/teacher meeting pending, and she fears it might get ugly. Her son has gotten another less-than-stellar grade on a homework assignment that ate an entire weekend and required the assistance of two adults with advanced degrees.

The latest assignment is just one of many that have taken their toll on my friend's family. In fact, she attributes the case of shingles she developed last year to a "Welcome to the New World" brochure that had to be typed and tri-folded (no cutting and pasting allowed). Despite repeated efforts to learn the intricacies of desktop publishing software, she and her son

Lisa Mangione, "Is Homework Working?," *Phi Delta Kappan*, vol. 89, no. 8, April 2008, pp. 614–615. Copyright © 2008 by Phi Delta Kappa International. All rights reserved. Reprinted with permission of Phi Delta Kappa International, www.pdkintl.org.

were unable to master the formatting. At 11:30 p.m., they admitted defeat and decided to submit the information typed, but in paragraph form, bracing themselves for the hit. Surprisingly, they still couldn't make this assignment go away. Deemed unacceptable by the teacher, it was handed back to the student, who was forced to outsource it to yet another adult.

Contemplating her case for the fateful meeting, my friend wonders aloud, "Am I being unreasonable?" In the depth of her sighs, I hear both outrage and defeat.

As a special education teacher (now termed "consultant teacher"), I do not routinely dole out grades, but I collaborate with my colleagues (the "general education" teachers) to design, facilitate, and evaluate instruction that is fair and appropriate for the students in question. Regardless of the assignment, I can ask my colleagues: What is the curricular goal? What is it you want them to know and understand? If the goal is to demonstrate an understanding of the reasons why immigrants came to America, then *how* that understanding is assessed can take myriad forms. A brochure? Sure! But *designing* the brochure should not become more important than the point of the brochure, as seemed to be the case with my friend's son.

For many teachers reading this, that idea does not come as a revelation. Many of us have received enough hours of professional development to earn another degree: asking "essential questions," adhering to "backwards design," and focusing on "process over product" are all part of our repertoire. We get it already.

Or do we? The more conversations I have with friends and relatives who are panicked and confused over the homework that their children receive (and are incapable of completing on their own), the more outraged I become. As a new parent, I wonder what position I'll take when my own daughter has a doozy of an assignment. Do I let her tackle it independently, even if it means she will stumble occasionally? Or will I succumb to the pressure of ensuring that she gets "good grades," even if those grades scarcely reflect any real understanding?

Students Should Be Able to Complete Homework Alone

The heart of the matter is this: Is this a parenting issue, or a school policy issue? In my own experience, my father, a veteran teacher, never once hovered over me as I did my homework (that is, when I did it). Admittedly, I was not always as dutiful and tenacious about it as he would have liked, but that was *my* work, and the grades were reflective of *my* output, not his. (I think it may have been the best parenting lesson I could have received.)

And what about those students who will not get help with their homework, simply because the adults at home are unable or unwilling to help? Should those students be penalized for a home environment that doesn't enforce—or, more accurately, *ensure*—that their grades stay "in the black"?

My father's position was that homework should be used to reinforce what was already modeled and taught.

If the responsibility rests with the source, would that be the school or the individual teacher? After all, homework is generally assigned and graded at the discretion of each teacher. In that regard, I still defer to the advice my father gave me when I was baffled over assigning and grading homework during my first year of teaching: "Homework should be independent practice," he said. And then—using a sports metaphor I could actually understand—he compared homework to the practice that athletes endure: they may mess up, but that's the point of practice. "After all," he continued, "it only counts in the game."

My father's position was that homework should be used to reinforce what was already modeled and taught. It should be met with guidance, never graded. Of course, that would require that it actually be done, which is why so many teachers feel it *must* be graded. How else, they argue, can you see that students do it? If that policy worked (using grades as both positive and negative reinforcers), then this entire discussion would be moot; grading would solve everything. Then again, if grades were not used as leverage and homework assignments solely provided an opportunity for reinforcement of newly learned concepts, then the quality of student performance would be tied to their efforts in practice. (They just better not miss practice.)

To be fair, not all teachers grade homework, and of those who do, not all of them necessarily grade it harshly. But the range of what constitutes a reasonable assignment is so far-reaching that "homework" is an entirely different animal from school to school, class to class, teacher to teacher, ranging from rote memorization of spelling words to long-term projects that encompass an entire unit of study. Given so broad a range, how can the grades be considered valid? What do they mean, anyway? A grade of 75 in Ms. Stickler's class—even if backed up by a rubric—is still likely to have a subjective slant. More important, if the work behind the scenes was actually the work of little elves (make that big parental elves), then the grade—on which so much hinges—has even less connection to the student's understanding.

Those Who Need Practice Most Are Not Doing the Homework

Still, even if grades were removed from the equation, it is doubtful that homework would suddenly become attractive to most students. Unfortunately, the students who most need the practice and discipline of self-guided assignments are the ones who just never do them. The fact that we continually penalize these students baffles me. During the school day, they are the ones for whom you stand on your head, devise rewards, and do whatever works—all in a futile attempt to motivate them. Still, we expect these same kids to skip home, plop down at a kitchen table (where I assume a wholesome snack of milk and cookies is waiting), and spend an additional two or three hours poring over what they refused to do earlier. Interesting logic. We may think that grading homework sends a message that it isn't optional, but the fact is, the students who are most at risk will almost always opt out.

So, if the kids who really need the practice aren't attempting the homework and are getting little support at home, and the ones who do complete it are often getting too much support, is homework working for anybody?

We may think that grading homework sends a message that it isn't optional, but the fact is, the students who are most at risk will almost always opt out.

While the debate over homework isn't new, it has resurfaced with some recent findings that there is a negative correlation between the time spent on homework and student achievement. In other words, there is a point of diminishing returns. According to Duke University professor Harris Cooper's research, elementary students get no academic benefit (other than reading practice), while middle and high school students see no gains beyond one-and-a-half to two hours per night. Arguably, the efficacy is not related exclusively to quantity but depends on quality. The real issue is, what are the kids spending that hour or two doing?

Cooper himself does not advocate banning homework altogether, even at the elementary level, but he does call for specific guidelines for school districts, teachers, and teacher training programs. And despite recommending a mix of "mandatory" and "voluntary" assignments, homework, he says, should not be graded. (Mandatory assignments that are missed would result in remediation, not a failing grade.) In addition, Cooper insists that parent involvement be minimal and geared mostly toward creating an "optimal environment for self-study."

I can't help but feel satisfied when I read Cooper's recommendations. The country's foremost researcher on the subject of homework confirms my own view. But can I really take credit for it? After all, I did have to ask my dad for help.

11

Special Education Homework Strategies Can Work for All Students

Sara Finegan

Sara Finegan lives and works in San Diego, California, where she teaches a special day class for fourth, fifth, and sixth graders. She has taught in the public and private school sectors for more than twenty-five years in both general and special education settings.

When it comes to homework, begin with the end in mind. Homework must have a purpose and be effective in building good study habits. Many of the strategies used for students with learning disabilities are the same strategies classroom teachers can and should use in deciding how and what to assign as homework. Decreasing the amount of homework can be the difference for some students in whether they even attempt to complete an assignment. Careful use of consequences and rewards is essential, and all homework should be about building competence as opposed to completing an endurance test.

I'm a big fan of homework, but it has to be meaningful homework, and it has to be customized to fit your learners and their current skill levels. Here are my thoughts about designing home practice in a demanding classroom:

It must be purposeful.

Homework for the sake of homework is detrimental to a struggling learner. Kids aren't stupid, and they know on some level, no matter how old they are, if you are just making work for them because you think that's what teachers are supposed to do.

The purpose of homework in a demanding classroom is to:

- *give the child additional practice in a newly learned concept or skill and*

- *to provide a structure for a task they should be doing on a regular basis.*

Homework for the sake of homework is detrimental to a struggling learner.

When it comes to additional practice, a demanding classroom teacher designs a set of practice problems or questions that address what was worked on that day in class. Examples might be: 5–10 addition problems; a set of similar word problems that require the child to set up an equation; comprehension questions that pertain to one or two plot features; practice making inferences based on short pieces of text.

There are some excellent workbooks available in stores and online that provide practice problems in many content areas. There are also some awful ones. I remember a child I worked with in an after-school program who had a reading homework packet that was obviously written in the 1960's: it was dry, pedantic, and completely uninteresting to me and the student.

A goal should be to establish a sense of competence.

I do not want my students to have their parents do their homework, spend hours with their child struggling to get it done, or to leave the kitchen table feeling utterly drained and unskilled.

I want my students to leave the homework table feeling like they get it, or are on the way to getting it. I want them to feel *able*. Now this is not going to happen all the time, particularly when we're learning new skill sets.

But if, over time, the student is confident that in general, he or she is going to be able to master the skills, or retain the information, or do the task fairly well, most kids will be willing to struggle a bit from time to time at home.

A Homework Routine Should Create Study Habits

Almost every school urges children to read for 30 minutes or more per day at home. Thirty minutes is a lot for a child who has little reading stamina, or who struggles mightily with decoding or comprehension. This kind of assignment, without any other components, isn't going to help a child with learning disabilities as much as it could with a few modifications.

If a child is not able to read for 30 minutes in class without losing focus or melting down, do not require it at home. Build stamina slowly. A student who can only read for three minutes should be given a 3–5 minute reading assignment for home, followed by a book on tape or a story a parent is willing to read out loud. (Reading homework is not always just about reading skill, but also about our relationship to text and how we think about stories—books on CD, tape or read aloud can do just fine.)

At a certain age and stage, kids can be taught how to write a reading response. This is an extremely important skill and needs to be built in layers, slowly, with lots of practice. The practice can be done at home, provided that you give the child examples to follow or a formula to use in the initial practice stages. In early grades, a reading response can be an illustration with two or three sentences about a character or your opinion about the book.

My fifth and sixth graders are currently, in the fall of the year, writing three-paragraph responses: a summary of what they read; a description of a character or the problem; a connection that they are making to the story or to a character. By the end of the year I hope they will be doing deeper thinking and writing, but we are taking it one step at a time. Right now, their daily reading homework includes writing the response (yes, daily, though at least one child dictates to his grandmother because the act of writing is driving him crazy) because I want it to become an automatic habit for them in preparation for middle school.

Nobody knows a child better than his or her parents, and we need to be responsive to them with regard to the work we send home.

As much as possible, coordinate, communicate, and negotiate with your partners: the parents.

We don't want parents doing the homework, but we want them to support it. Nobody knows a child better than his or her parents, and we need to be responsive to them with regard to the work we send home.

Right now, I have a couple of students who have major difficulties with attention. One of them has autism and ADHD [Attention Deficit Hyperactivity Disorder]; the other has ADHD. Both of them have parents who are excellent about notifying me when homework is just too much. In these kinds of cases, we need to make *accommodations* and reduce the amount of homework in one or more ways.

- We might limit the number of problems to solve on a math set, or require less reading.

- We might change the type of work to be done. Multiple choice or short-answer, fill-in-the-blank homework works better for these kids than other kinds of comprehension or social studies assignments.

- We might change the way the homework needs to be done. Both of my students are allowed to dictate their reading responses to a parent or grandparent, because getting them to sit down and write after school, when meds are wearing off and the brain is tired is not going to be a pleasant experience.

- We might give choices. One of my students, who has moderately functioning autism, fought homework at home for a long time. When he came to my classroom, I provided three to four tasks to be done at home— and instructed him to pick two. This gives him the power over the work, not me over him, and has made him voluntarily do his homework, without difficulty, when he gets home.

Homework Should Build Self-Discipline

I don't want my students' parents to spend hours fighting with their kids to get work done. I also don't want students neglecting their home practice. Home practice needs to become a routine, a habit.

In a demanding classroom, this is done with incentives as well as consequences.

An immediate, automatic, small reward needs to be given to kids with learning disabilities when they turn in their homework. As homework is checked in, kids can receive a sticker, a punch on "daily work index card", a raffle ticket (dollar store prizes at a drawing once a week or every two weeks) or some other desired privilege. It should be automatic and not served with effusive praise unless the child has a history of not turning in homework, in which case positive comments are a good re-enforcement.

If you have other students check in homework, kids will be far more invested in getting it done. It's hard to face a teacher or aide and explain why homework was not done, but for some reason it's even harder to face your peers when all of them have been working hard. This can be especially true if there's a class-wide reward for 100% homework turned in, a ploy I use every now and then ($5 pizzas from Little Caesars work every time). In general, the incentives should be small and cheap.

Home practice needs to become a routine, a habit.

Consequences Are More Complicated

The traditional "you miss recess" consequence is not a good idea in most special education classrooms, where kids need to get outside and move around as a kinesthetic break from the intellectual activity you're piling on.

I've been experimenting with a form letter that goes home, filled out by the student, for parents to read and sign. It's on bright orange paper, and can't be missed by anyone coming even close to a backpack, and it requires the student to acknowledge work that wasn't done and ask for help creating a plan to do it. I keep all of them in my students' portfolio folders, and it's a great visual—neon orange is eye-catching.

Restriction of free time until the homework is made up is a pretty good consequence, though again, many students, particularly those with autism or who have sensory issues need to have some minutes of free time between tasks in order to keep their minds working well.

I'm inclined to use restriction from weekly class-wide fun activities as a consequence for not doing homework. If the last ½ hour of class on Friday is reserved for cupcakes or a great game, kids who didn't do homework during the week can sit in another classroom or in the office to make up their work.

The combination of incentives and meaningful but not devastating consequences in a demanding classroom helps students learn good work habits at home and in school.

12

Life Lessons Are More Important Than School Lessons

John Taylor Gatto

John Taylor Gatto is a former New York State and New York City Teacher of the Year and the author of several books on compulsory education. His most recent book, published in 2010, is titled Weapons of Mass Instruction: A Schoolteacher's Journey Through the Dark World of Compulsory Schooling.

There is far more to an education than what happens in school. There is more to learning than memorizing facts and taking achievement tests. Today's schooling makes few demands on students to pursue real achievement, instead relying on worksheets and homework and constant testing as substitutes for the mastery of skills needed to be truly successful in life. Families and students can fight back against the obstacles institutionalized schooling can present by using curiosity and creativity to encourage independent thought.

Nobody *gives* you an education. If you want one, you have to take it.

Only you can educate you—and you can't do it by memorizing. You have to find out who you are by experience and by risk-taking, then pursue your own nature intensely. School routines are set up to discourage you from self-discovery. People who know who they are make trouble for schools.

To know yourself, you have to keep track of your random choices, figure out your patterns, and use this knowledge to dominate your own mind. It's the only way that free will can grow. If you avoid this, other minds will manipulate and control you lifelong.

School routines are set up to discourage you from self-discovery.

One method people use to find out who they are becoming, before others do, is to keep a journal, where they log what attracts their attention, along with some commentary. In this way, you get to listen to yourself instead of listening only to others.

Another path to self-discovery that seems to have atrophied through schooling lies in finding a mentor. People aren't the only mentors. Books can serve as mentors if you learn to read intensely, with every sense alert to nuances. Books can change your life, as mentors do.

I experienced precious little of such thinking in 30 years of teaching in the public junior high schools of Manhattan's ultra-progressive Upper West Side [New York]. I was by turns amused, disgusted, and disbelieving when confronted with the curriculum—endless drills of fractions and decimals, reading assignments of science fiction, [American author] Jack London, and one or two [William] Shakespeare plays for which the language had been simplified. The strategy was to kill time and stave off the worst kinds of boredom that can lead to trouble—the trouble that comes from being made aware that you are trapped in irrelevancy and powerless to escape.

Institutionalized schooling, I gradually realized, is about obedience in exchange for favors and advantages: Sit where I tell you, speak when I allow it, memorize what I've told you to memorize. Do these things, and I'll take care to put you above your classmates.

Wouldn't you think everyone could figure out that school "achievement tests" measure no achievement that common sense would recognize? The surrender required of students meets the primary duty of bureaucratic establishment: to protect established order.

It wasn't always this way. Classical schooling—the kind I was lucky enough to have growing up—teaches independent thought, appreciation for great works, and an experience of the world not found within the confines of a classroom. It was an education that is missing in public schools today but still exists in many private schools—and can for you and your children, too, if you take time to learn how to learn.

Wouldn't you think everyone could figure out that school "achievement tests" measure no achievement that common sense would recognize?

A Small Town Integrates Hands-On Learning to Enrich Achievement

In the fall of 2009, a documentary film will be released by a resident of my hometown of Monongahela, Pennsylvania. Laura Magone's film, *One Extraordinary Street*, centers on a two-mile-long road that parallels polluted Pigeon Creek. Park Avenue, as it's called, is on the wrong side of the tracks in this little-known coal-mining burg of 4,500 souls.

So far Park Avenue has produced an Army chief of staff, the founder of the Disney Channel, the inventor of the Nerf football, the only professional baseball player to ever strike out all 27 enemy batsmen in a nine-inning game, a winner of the National Book Award, a respected cardiologist, Hall of Fame quarterback Joe Montana, and the writer whose words you're reading.

Did the education Monongahela offered make all these miracles possible? I don't know. It was an education filled with hands-on experience, including cooking the school meals, serving them individually (not cafeteria-style) on tablecloths, and cleaning up afterward. Students handled the daily maintenance, including basic repairs. If you weren't earning money and adding value to the town by the age of seven, you were considered a jerk. I swept out a printing office daily, sold newspapers, shoveled snow, cut grass, and sold lemonade.

Classical schooling isn't psychologically driven. The ancient Greeks discovered thousands of years ago that rules and ironclad procedures, when taken too seriously, burn out imagination, stifle courage, and wipe the leadership clean of resourcefulness. Greek education was much more like play, with studies undertaken for their own sake, to satisfy curiosity. It assumed that sane children want to grow up and recognized that childhood ends much earlier than modern society typically allows.

We read [Julius] Caesar's *Gallic Wars*—in translation between fifth and seventh grades and, for those who wanted, in Latin in ninth and tenth grades. Caesar was offered to us not as some historical relic but as a workshop in dividing and conquering superior enemies. We read *The Odyssey* [by Homer] as an aid to thinking about the role of family in a good life, as the beating heart of meaning.

Greek education was much more like play, with studies undertaken for their own sake, to satisfy curiosity.

Monongahela's education integrated students, from first grade on, into the intimate life and culture of the town. Its classrooms were free of the familiar tools of official pedagogy—dumbed-down textbooks, massively irrelevant standardized tests, insanely slowed-down sequences. It was an education rich in relationships, tradition, and respect for the best that's been written. It was a growing-up that demanded real achievement.

The admissions director at Harvard College told *The New York Times* a few years ago that Harvard admits only students with a record of distinctive accomplishment. I instantly thought of the Orwellian [referring to the writings of George Orwell] newspeak at my own Manhattan school where achievement tests were the order of the day. What achievement? Like the noisy royalty who intimidated Alice until her head cleared and she realized they were only a pack of cards, school achievement is just a pack of words.

Challenging the System Is Hard but Worth the Effort

As a schoolteacher, I was determined to act as a deliberate saboteur, and so for 30 years I woke up committed to making the system hurt in some small way and to changing the destiny of children in my orbit in a large way.

Without the eclectic grounding in classical training that I had partially absorbed, neither goal would have been possible. I set out to use the classical emphasis on qualities and specific powers. I collected from every kid a list of three powers they felt they already possessed and three weaknesses they might like to remedy in the course of the school year.

I pledged to them that I'd do my level best inside the limitations the institution imposed to make time, advice, and support available toward everyone's private goals. There would be group lessons as worthwhile as I could come up with, but my priorities were the opportunities outside the room, outside the school, even outside the city, to strengthen a power or work on a weakness.

I let a 13-year-old boy who dreamed of being a comic-book writer spend a week in the public library—with the assistance of the librarian—to learn the tricks of graphic storytelling. I sent a shy 13-year-old girl in the company of a loudmouth classmate to the state capitol—she to speak to her local legislator, he to teach her how to be fearless. Today, that shy girl is a trial attorney.

If you understand where a kid wants to go—the kid has to understand that first—it isn't hard to devise exercises, complete with academics, that can take them there.

But school often acts as an obstacle to success. To go from the confinement of early childhood to the confinement of the classroom to the confinement of homework, working to amass a record entitling you to a "good" college, where the radical reduction of your spirit will continue, isn't likely to build character or prepare you for a good life.

I quit teaching in 1991 and set out to discover where this destructive institution had come from, why it had taken the shape it had, how it managed to beat back its many critics for a century while growing bigger and more intrusive, and what we might do about it.

School does exactly what it was created to do: It solves, or at least mitigates, the problem of a restless, ambitious labor pool, so deadly for capitalist economies; and it confronts democracy's other deadly problem—that ordinary people might one day learn to un-divide themselves, band together in the common interest, and take control of the institutions that shape their lives.

School often acts as an obstacle to success.

The present system of institutionalized schooling is a product of two or three centuries of economic and political thinking that spread primarily from a militaristic state in the dis-united Germanies known as Prussia. That philosophy destroyed classical training for the common people, reserving it for those who were expected to become leaders. Education, in the words of famous economists (such as William Playfair), captains of industry (Andrew Carnegie), and even a man who would be president (Woodrow Wilson), was a means of keeping the middle and lower classes in line and of keeping the engines of capitalism running.

In a 1909 address to New York City teachers, Wilson, then president of Princeton University, said, "We want one class of persons to have a liberal education, and we want another class of persons, a very much larger class of necessity to forgo the privilege of a liberal education."

My job isn't to indict Woodrow or anyone else, only to show you how inevitable the schools you hate must be in the economy and social order we're stuck with. Liberal education served the ancient Greeks well until they got too rich to allow it, just as it served America the same way until we got too rich to allow it.

Success Does Not Depend on Formal Schooling

You can make the system an offer it can't refuse by doing small things, individually. You can publicly oppose—in writing, in speech, in actions—anything that will perpetuate the institution as it is. The accumulated weight of your resistance and disapproval, together with that of thousands more, will erode the energy of any bureaucracy.

You can calmly refuse to take standardized tests. Follow the lead of [Herman] Melville's moral genius in *Bartleby, the Scrivener*, and ask everyone, politely, to write: "I prefer not to take this test" on the face of the test packet.

You can, of course, homeschool or unschool. You can inform your kids that bad grades won't hurt them at all in life, if they actually learn to master valuable skills and put them on offer to the world at large. And you can begin to free yourself from the conditioned fear that not being accepted at a "good" college will preclude you from a comfortable life. If the lack of a college degree didn't stop Steve Jobs (Apple), Bill Gates (Microsoft), Michael Dell (Dell Computer), Larry Ellison (Oracle), Ingvar Kamprad (IKEA), Warren Avis (Avis Rent-a-Car), Ted Turner (CNN), and so many others, then it shouldn't be too hard for you to see that you've been bamboozled, flummoxed, played for a sap by the propaganda mills of schooling. Get rid of your assumptions.

If you are interested in education, I've tried to show you a little about how that's done, and I have faith you can learn the rest on your own. Schooling operates out of an assumption that ordinary people are biologically or psychologically or politically inferior; education assumes that individuals are sovereign spirits. Societies that don't know that need to be changed or broken.

Once you take responsibility for your own education, you'll join a growing army of men and women all across America who are waking up to the mismatch schools inflict on the young—a mismatch between what common sense tells you they'll need to know, and what is actually taught. You'll have the exquisite luxury of being able to adapt to conditions, to opportunities, to the particular spirits of your kids. With you as educational czar or czarina, feedback becomes your friend and guide.

I've traveled 3 million miles to every corner of this country and 12 others, and believe me, people everywhere are gradually waking up and striking out in new directions. Don't wait for the government to say it's OK, just come on in—the water's fine.

13

There Is Room for Improvement in America's Approach to Education

Mark Schneider

Mark Schneider is vice president for new educational initiatives at the American Institutes for Research and a distinguished professor of political science at the State University of New York. He served as commissioner of education statistics at the US Department of Education from 2005 to 2008.

The 2009 High School Transcript Study conducted by the National Center for Education Statistics revealed some interesting facts. The level of difficulty of a student's course load corresponded to the scores that student achieved on national achievement tests. The tougher the courses the higher the test scores, reflecting what should be obvious to all—hard work does pay off. Unfortunately, high schools are not taking advantage of this data to aggressively promote a more demanding academic schedule for their students. Nor are they pursuing opportunities that would afford more flexibility for students to increase their workload such as online courses and increased summer time options. The failure of schools to capitalize on this study's information to increase student proficiency should not be accepted.

Last week [April 2011] the National Center for Education Statistics released the latest High School Transcript Study, which presents information from transcripts collected from a nationally representative sample of more than 37,000 high school graduates from more than 700 public and private schools. The study documents the number and types of courses that high school graduates in the class of 2009 took and how their course-taking patterns relate to their performance on the 2009 National Assessment of Educational Progress (NAEP) mathematics and science assessments.

These transcript studies contain lots of interesting information. Here are some highlights.

For years now, many critics of education reform have complained about "narrowing the curriculum"—how only tested subjects get taught. Since No Child Left Behind [Act of 2001] focused on core academic disciplines such as reading and math, critics have argued that the curriculum focused on these subjects to the exclusion of others. *Wrong*—at least when it comes to high schools.

The transcript study shows a long-term trend in which high school students are taking more courses and more academic ones than ever before—a trend that shows no sign of abating. In short, the high school curriculum, far from narrowing, is getting deeper and broader.

Students who took a rigorous curricula outscored students who took a below-standard curriculum by more than 40 scale points in math and science.

For example, the number of high school credits graduates took has increased by 15 percent since 1990 (up from 23.6 in 1990 to 27.2 in 2009). This increase was driven by an emphasis on academics. Between 1990 and 2009, high school graduates increased their enrollment in "core academic" courses (English, math, science, and social studies) by 17 percent and in "other academic" courses (fine arts, foreign languages, and computer-related studies) by almost 50 percent. In contrast, students took fewer "other" courses (such as vocational education and personal hygiene). It is harder to sustain such large increases in credits as the base course load gets bigger, but still there was a 4 percent gain in credits taken since 2000. Again, this was driven by academic courses. Since 2000, students took one additional credit in "core academic" courses, an additional 0.5 credits in "other academic" courses, and continued to take fewer "other" courses.

A second important finding in the study is that a more rigorous curriculum pays off with higher NAEP science and math scores. Students who took a rigorous curricula outscored students who took a below-standard curriculum by more than 40 scale points in math and science. Clearly, this is correlational and not causal. The study shows that the relationship between curriculum and performance has persistent race and ethnicity patterns. At any level of curriculum, black and Hispanic students lag, often considerably, behind whites and Asian/Pacific Islanders.

This leads me to question the quality of the curriculum as delivered in schools serving minority students. I suspect that many schools are likely relabeling courses and not delivering the course content implied by the course titles. NAEP is undertaking some studies that should shed light on this issue.

Schools Fall Short in Embracing True Reform

Besides this race and ethnic difference, a couple of other issues strike me as important.

While there has been progress in getting more students to take a more rigorous course of study, far too few students are taking the most rigorous curriculum. Only about 13 percent of students take the "rigorous" curriculum, up from 10 percent in 2000 and 5 percent in 1990, but still a low number. More encouraging: 46 percent take the midlevel curriculum and the percentage of students with that curriculum continues to expand.

But perhaps most disturbing is that high schools are failing to exploit emerging opportunities for students to increase their course-taking. Many critics argue that our school year and school day are too short—and clearly the evidence from the transcript study shows that exposure to more courses is associated with higher NAEP scores. The transcript study explores two ways in which students could take more courses: summer school and online education. In both cases, our high schools are dropping the ball.

The transcript study shows that summer school is mostly for remediation and for students trying to recover from failing courses. For example, more than 30 percent of students who were in the least rigorous curriculum enrolled in summer school, while only 16 percent of the students who took the most rigorous curriculum did so. And students who enrolled in summer school scored far lower on NAEP math and science scores than did students who did not enroll in summer school. Clearly, enrollment in summer school is not usually for academic advancement.

> *Perhaps most disturbing is that high schools are failing to exploit emerging opportunities for students to increase their course-taking.*

Even more serious is our failure to take advantage of online education. Our ability to deliver high quality online math courses is far more advanced than in other subjects. Yet only 5 percent or so of students took online math courses—and they scored *lower* on their NAEP tests than students who did not take such courses. This suggests that like summer school, online education is more for credit recovery than for learning and perfecting advanced skills.

Online courses should allow good students to enhance their skills and take advanced courses that might not be available in their own school. Instead, our high schools are missing an opportunity for true advances in delivering high quality courses, not just for students who are lagging, but for students who want to excel.

Organizations to Contact

The editors have compiled the following list of organizations concerned with the issues debated in this book. The descriptions are derived from materials provided by the organizations. All have publications or information available for interested readers. The list was compiled on the date of publication of the present volume; the information provided here may change. Be aware that many organizations take several weeks or longer to respond to inquiries, so allow as much time as possible.

Alliance for Excellent Education
1201 Connecticut Ave. NW, Suite 901, Washington, DC   20036
(202) 828-0828 • fax: (202) 828-0821
website: www.all4ed.org

The Alliance for Excellent Education envisions a nation where all children graduate from high school with the knowledge and intellectual and social skills necessary for postsecondary learning and success in life. It publishes the biweekly newsletter, *Straight A's: Public Education Policy and Progress*, along with numerous reports on issues and policy.

Center on Reinventing Public Education (CRPE)
University of Washington Bothell, Seattle, WA   98195
(206) 685-2214 • fax: (206) 221-7402
e-mail: crpe@u.washington.edu
website: www.crpe.org

CRPE engages in independent research and policy analysis on a range of K-12 public education reform issues, including school choice, productivity, teachers, urban district reform, leadership, and state and federal reform. CRPE's work is based on two premises: that public schools should be measured against the goal of educating all children well, and that current institutions too often fail to achieve this goal. Its research, including *Limited Capacity at the State Level: A Threat to Fu-*

ture School Improvement, published in June 2011, seeks to understand complicated problems and to design innovative and practical solutions.

Challenge Success
485 Lasuen Mall, Stanford, CA   94305-3096
e-mail: info@challengesuccess.org
website: www.challengesuccess.org

Challenge Success, a project of the Stanford University School of Education, is a research-based intervention program focused on three core areas: school reform, parent education, and youth development. It works with parents, schools, and youth to encourage development of the skills for success that are often overlooked in the current system—critical thinking, character, creativity, resilience, self-management, and engagement with learning—while lessening the impact of the high stress, pressure-without-purpose environment in which students struggle.

Education Sector
1201 Connecticut Ave. NW, Suite 850, Washington, DC   20036
(202) 552-2840 • fax: (202) 775-5877
website: www.educationsector.org

Education Sector is an independent think tank that challenges conventional thinking in education policy. It is a nonprofit, nonpartisan organization committed to achieving a measurable impact in education policy, both by improving existing reform initiatives and by developing new, innovative solutions to the nation's most pressing education problems. Its website includes a section titled *Charts You Can Trust* that provides graphical presentations of research such as "Debt to Degree: A New Way of Measuring College Success," published in August 2011.

Education Trust
1250 H St. NW, Suite 700, Washington, DC   20005
(202) 293-1217 • fax: (202) 293-2605
website: www.edtrust.org

The Education Trust promotes high academic achievement for all students at all levels—pre-kindergarten through college. Its goal is to work alongside educators, parents, students, policy-makers, and civic and business leaders in communities across the country, providing practical assistance in their efforts to transform schools and colleges into institutions that serve all students well. Its April 2011 white paper, "Stuck Schools Revisited: Beneath the Averages," explores why current efforts are not enough to raise achievement and close performance gaps.

Thomas B. Fordham Institute

1016 16th St. NW, 8th Floor, Washington, DC 20036
(202) 223-5452 • fax: (202) 223-9226
e-mail: thegadfly@edexcellence.net
website: www.edexcellence.net

The Thomas B. Fordham Institute is a nonprofit think tank dedicated to advancing educational excellence in America's K-12 schools. The institute promotes policies that strengthen accountability and expand education options for parents and families. Its reports examine issues such as the No Child Left Behind Act, school choice, and teacher quality. The organization's *Flypaper Blog* provides engaging discussion about "ideas that stick."

Institute for Democratic Education in America (IDEA)

PO Box 452, Tarrytown, NY 10591
(800) 878-5740
e-mail: info@democraticeducation.org
website: http://democraticeducation.org

IDEA is a national nonprofit organization whose mission is to ensure that all young people can engage meaningfully with their education and gain the tools to build a just, democratic, and sustainable world. Founded by educators from across the country, IDEA is committed to bridging the disconnect between democratic values and the way society educates and treats young people. Its website features *The Eduvation Library*, a collaborative project to curate high quality resources that support meaningful learning and help build the will for change.

National Center for Education Statistics (NCES)
990 K St. NW, Washington, DC 20006
(202) 502-7300
website: http://nces.ed.gov

NCES is the primary federal entity responsible for collecting and analyzing data related to education in the United States and other nations. NCES is located within the US Department of Education and the Institute of Education Sciences. It fulfills a congressional mandate to collect, collate, analyze, and report complete statistics on the condition of American education; conduct and publish reports; and review and report on education activities internationally. The NCES website contains numerous reports and search tools useful in locating performance data for specific schools.

National Education Association (NEA)
1201 16th St. NW, Washington, DC 20036-3290
(202) 833-4000 • fax: (202) 822-7974
website: www.nea.org

The mission of the NEA is to advocate for education professionals and to unite its members and the nation to fulfill the promise of public education to prepare every student to succeed in a diverse and interdependent world. Its 3.2 million members include educators at all levels of public education in America. The NEA website provides its members with tools and ideas on topics such as classroom management and teaching strategies, while also keeping them informed on relevant topics and issues such as legislative action, educational funding, and more.

Rethinking Schools
1001 E Keefe Ave., Milwaukee, WI 53212
(414) 964-9646 • fax: (414) 964-7220
e-mail: office@rethinkingschools.org
website: www.rethinkingschools.org

Rethinking Schools began as a local effort to address issues such as standardized testing and a textbook-dominated curriculum. It is firmly committed to the vision that public education is central to the creation of a humane, caring, multira-cial democracy. It publishes the quarterly magazine, *Rethinking Schools*, available on its website.

Bibliography

Books

Richard Arum
and Josipa Roksa

Academically Adrift: Limited Learning on College Campuses. Chicago: University of Chicago Press, 2011.

Sara Bennett and
Nancy Kalish

The Case Against Homework: How Homework Is Hurting Children and What Parents Can Do About It. New York: Three Rivers Press, 2006.

Amy Chua

Battle Hymn of the Tiger Mother. New York: Penguin Press, 2011.

David T. Conley

College Knowledge: What It Really Takes for Students to Succeed and What We Can Do to Get Them Ready. San Francisco, CA: Jossey-Bass, 2005.

Harris Cooper

The Battle Over Homework: Common Ground for Administrators, Teachers, and Parents. Thousand Oaks, CA: Corwin Press, 2007.

William Crain

Reclaiming Childhood: Letting Children Be Children in Our Achievement-Oriented Society. New York: Henry Holt and Company, 2003.

Howard Gardner

Five Minds for the Future. Cambridge, MA: Harvard Business School Press, 2009.

John Taylor Gatto *Weapons of Mass Instruction: A Schoolteacher's Journey Through the Dark World of Compulsory Schooling.* British Columbia, Canada: New Society Publishers, 2010.

Frederick M. Hess *The Same Thing Over and Over: How School Reformers Get Stuck in Yesterday's Ideas.* Cambridge, MA: Harvard University Press, 2010.

Alfie Kohn *Feel Bad Education: And Other Contrarian Essays on Children and Schooling.* Boston: Beacon Press, 2011.

Alfie Kohn *The Homework Myth: Why Our Kids Get Too Much of a Bad Thing.* Cambridge, MA: Da Capo Lifelong Books, 2007.

Etta Kralovec and *The End of Homework: How* John Buell *Homework Disrupts Families, Overburdens Children, and Limits Learning.* Boston: Beacon Press, 2000.

Charles M. Payne *So Much Reform, So Little Change: The Persistence of Failure in Urban Schools.* Cambridge, MA: Harvard University Press, 2008.

Daniel H. Pink *Drive: The Surprising Truth About What Motivates Us.* New York: Riverhead Books, 2009.

James Taylor *Positive Pushing: How to Raise a Successful and Happy Child.* New York: Hyperion, 2002.

Cathy Vatterott — *Rethinking Homework: Best Practices That Support Diverse Needs.* Alexandria, VA: Association for Supervision & Curriculum Development, 2009.

Tony Wagner — *The Global Achievement Gap: Why Even Our Best Schools Don't Teach the New Survival Skills Our Children Need—And What We Can Do About It.* New York: Basic Books, 2008.

Periodicals and Internet Sources

Patrice Apodaca — "Are We Sending Kids on a 'Race to Nowhere'?," *Daily Pilot*, April 26, 2011.

Richard Arum and Josipa Roksa — "College, Too Easy for Its Own Good," *Los Angeles Times*, June 3, 2011.

Lawrence Baines — "Learning from the World: Achieving More by Doing Less," *Phi Delta Kappan*, October 2007.

Samantha Brix — "Do We Put Too Much Pressure on High School Students?," *North Shore Sun*, April 12, 2011.

Amy Chua — "Why Chinese Mothers Are Superior," *The Wall Street Journal*, January 8, 2011.

Sam Dillon — "High School Classes May Be Advanced in Name Only," *New York Times*, April 25, 2009.

Ellen Gamerman   "What Makes Finnish Kids So
                  Smart?," *The Wall Street Journal*,
                  February 29, 2008.

Michael E.   "Spare the Rigor, Spoil the Learning,"
Gordon and   *Academe Online*, July/August 2010.
Oded Palmon   www.aaup.org.

Chris Irvine   "UK's Biggest School to Scrap
                  Homework," *The Telegraph*,
                  September 28, 2008.

John Keilman   "Online Learning for Illinois High
                  Schoolers Inspires Praise, Suspicion,"
                  Chicago Tribune, April 24, 2011.

Stacy Teicher   "NAEP Report: 'Rigor Works,' So
Khadaroo   Schools Need Tougher Classes,"
                  Christian Science Monitor, April 13,
                  2011.

Alfie Kohn   "Changing the Homework Default,"
                  Independent School Magazine, Winter
                  2007.

Josh Linkner   "How Teachers Can Save Our Kids,"
                  JoshLinkner.com, May 2, 2011.
                  www.joshlinker.com.

Jonathan Martin   "Blame Schools, Not Students, for
                  'Failure of School Reform,'"
                  Connected Principals, September 19,
                  2010.

Jay Mathews   "Inside the AP Testing Debate,"
                  Newsweek, June 13, 2010.

Shannon Moriarty	"Homeless with Homework," Change.org, March 3, 2009. www.change.org.
Sharon Otterman	"At One School, a Push for More Playtime," *New York Times*, January 12, 2011.
Denise Pope	"Beyond 'Doing School': From 'Stressed-Out' to 'Engaged in Learning,'" *Education Canada*, Summer 2011.
Robert J. Samuelson	"School Reform's Meager Results," *The Washington Post*, September 6, 2010.
Jonathan Schorr and Deborah McGriff	"Future Schools," *EducationNext*, Summer 2011. www.education next.org.
Melanie Smolin	"The Homework Dilemma: How Much Is Too Much?," Takepart.com, January 14, 2011. www.takepart.com.
James Taylor	"Teach Your Children to Suck It Up," *San Francisco Examiner*, March 16, 2011.
Beth Teitell	"Homework Hell," *Boston Globe*, May 2, 2010.
Cathy Vatterott	"Five Hallmarks of Good Homework," *Educational Leadership*, September 2010.
Kelly Vaughan	"NPR: How Much Homework Is Too Much?," *Gotham Schools*, September 12, 2008. www.gothamschools.org.

Index

Homework rewards
   behavioral, 53–56
   learning disabilities and,
      80–81
   motivation vs., 9, 74

I

Indiana University, 27
The Internet, 26

J

Japan, homework practices, 50
Jefferson, Thomas, 21
Jones, Elizabeth, 11, 17, 18, 22
Journaling, 15, 84

K

Kalish, Nancy, 13–14, 21, 63–69
Kansas University, 31
Keith, Timothy, 56
King, Audrey, 68–69
Kino School, Tucson, Arizona, 23
Kinzie, Jillian, 27, 30
Kohn, Alfie
   academic ability, 13–15
   competition in learning, 18
   educational mindset, 15–16
   excessive homework, 22–23
   homework research needed,
      52–58
Krause, Tom, 17

L

LeTendre, Gerald, 50
Life lessons, importance of
   challenging the system, 87–89
   hands-on learning, 85–87

   overview, 83–85
   success and, 89–90
Love, Allegra, 15
Low-income student concerns, 43,
   53–54

M

Magone, Laura, 85–87
Mandatory homework, 74–75
Mangione, Lisa, 70–75
Marks, Mindy, 25, 28–31
Mathews, Jay, 41–43
Melville, Herman, 89
Mental health concerns of stu-
   dents, 37–38, 40
Minority student concerns, 93
Misconceptions over homework,
   13–15
Montana, Joe, 85
Montessori schools, 54
Motivation
   homework influence, 56
   outside motivation, 61–62
   rewards vs., 9, 74
   rote memorization and, 48
   self-motivation, 26
   sleep deprivation and, 20
   student health and, 38

N

Narrowing the curriculum, 92
A Nation at Risk (National Com-
   mission on Excellence in
   Education), 16
National Assessment of Educa-
   tional Progress (NAEP), 7, 92–94
National Center for Education
   Statistics, 91–95

T